Dr. Stanley Pearle

A MAN OF
VISION

As told to Cara Lopez Lee

ARBOR
AB
BOOKS

Book design by:

Arbor Books, Inc.
www.arborbooks.com

Printed in Canada

Dr. Stanley Pearle: A Man of Vision
Dr. Stanley Pearle
1. Title 2. Author 3. Biography

Library of Congress Control Number: 2006937595

ISBN 10: 0-9790469-1-2
ISBN 13: 978-0-9790469-1-9

Table of Contents

Introduction

DR. STANLEY PEARLE STARTED A REVOLUTION.

It began in 1961, with one small office and five employees in Savannah, Georgia. The place was called Pearle Optical, and it paved the way for a new kind of business.

Dr. Pearle kept the premise simple, offering three basic services: professional optometry, prescription filling by his company's own lab and the largest selection of frames in town. He later expanded on that equation to include convenient locations, longer hours, friendly service and low prices—a combination he simply called "value."

Many of Dr. Pearle's ideas had been tried before, but he always believed in learning from the success of others. A humble man, he simply tied up all the best ideas he'd seen into a new package, signed his name to it and presented it to the public.

That alone would have earned Dr. Pearle success. But what made him a true innovator in the worlds of optometry and retail was the nationwide scope of his vision. He was the first to create an optical company on such a large scale, with a unified image and countrywide advertising.

Pearle Optical grew into Pearle Vision, a company that

truly stood alone for the first 20 years of its existence. Today, after more than 40 years in business, the name is still highly recognized by most American consumers, whether they need eyewear or not.

These days, many optometric companies offer low-cost, full-service, one-stop eye care shopping, but almost all of them are based on concepts that Dr. Pearle made popular: convenient and attractive shopping locations, friendly service and a large selection of fashionable products.

Dr. Pearle knew his popular business model would never have taken off if he hadn't understood one very important principle. "There's no question in my mind," he said, "that the better staff you have, the more success you have. And if you have a second rate staff, you don't prosper. We always recognized that people were the most important aspect of the service we were offering."

Dr. Pearle believed in creating what he called a "culture of friendly service." It wasn't easy, but in the beginning—and in the end—it was clear that he himself was the key to the idea's success.

To all those who have known Dr. Pearle, there was never a nicer guy in the world of business. He has been a mentor to many—family, friends, colleagues and employees alike. His personal dedication to integrity, friendliness and quality service has always made itself felt throughout the company he created, even after his retirement.

Dr. Pearle's ability to imbue an entire company with his own personal ethics is an enviable achievement. In the competitive world of American business, cynicism can easily take over as businesses struggle to get ahead—and stay ahead—at any cost.

But this has never been Dr. Pearle's way. His achievements have sent a hopeful message to everyone who wishes to make a mark in the world: that the greatest success comes from refusing to compromise your values.

Chapter 1

Humble Beginnings

LONG BEFORE HE BECAME AMERICA'S BEST-KNOWN optometrist, Stanley Pearle was simply a boy called "Buddy." He doesn't remember anymore why he had that nickname, but even now, at the age of 88, his blue eyes still hold a trace of that irrepressibly friendly and optimistic kid.

This happy attitude didn't come from an easy life, however. His father, Goodman Pearle, left the family early on, deserting his young wife Dorothy and leaving her alone with their three-year-old son Lester, as well as the soon-to-be-born Stanley and his fraternal twin, Merle. They arrived on October 12, 1918, and remained inseparable throughout their childhood.

The brothers rarely saw their father. Goodman was a successful haberdasher in town and Merle and Stanley spotted him on the street once or twice, though they never really talked about him.

Older brother Lester had a lot of difficulty dealing with the situation, however, especially when his mother would send him to pick up a late child support check on occasion. Lester looked exactly like his father, too; Stanley was always aware how much growing up without a dad affected his older brother.

But Stanley himself refused to suffer over a man he never knew.

"Didn't know him, didn't care to know him," he said. "I didn't have much interest in finding out more because as far as I was concerned, I wasn't interested in him."

He wasn't an unfeeling young man, nor was he in denial. He simply always had a gift for noticing what was right in his life and putting the emphasis on that, rather than on what was wrong.

Also, he had two uncles, Phil and Dave, as well as a grandmother who watched over him along with his mother. By all his own accounts, Stanley had a wonderful childhood and didn't miss out on a thing.

Buddy, Merle, their two uncles and their mother all lived in his grandma's skinny, three-story house in a working class neighborhood of Pittsburgh, Pennsylvania. Grandma was an immigrant, a Russian Jew who occasionally made traditional foods like stuffed cabbage, and encouraged her grandchildren to play music.

Stanley knew her as a strong, warm-hearted but not entirely conventional woman.

"She smoked a cigars," he said. "She had asthma and for some reason, she believed that a stogie was good for it."

In contrast, he remembers his mother as a pretty, lively young woman who could easily have remarried—and Stanley never understood why she didn't.

As for Dorothy's brothers, Uncle Phil was a tough-talking, no-nonsense cop and Uncle Dave was a gentle-hearted guy who owned a men's secondhand clothing store. Uncle Dave ran illegal poker games in the back room most weekends, which his brother politely ignored.

Each of these characters played an important role in Stanley's upbringing, and in the formation of his strong personal code of ethics, which included a great deal of family loyalty and a genuine interest in humanity. From early on, he was, as they say, a people person.

Life Scout

HE ALSO SEEMED TO BE A NATURAL LEADER—a skill he uncovered while in the Boy Scouts. He joined when he was 11, along with his brother Merle, and it became such an important part of his life that he even thought about pursuing forestry as a career.

The troop meetings were held far across town, and getting to them was no small undertaking. The family didn't have a car, so the boys had to take a couple of streetcars—which only got them so far. Their scoutmaster would always meet them *en route* and drive them the rest of the way.

They could have joined a closer troop, but an older friend of theirs was a patrol leader for the more distant one, and he vowed that his scoutmaster was the best. Even then, Stanley was willing to go a little out of his way for quality. To him, the trip was worth it because he wanted to have a scout leader he could look up to.

Scouting taught Stanley a resourcefulness that he might not have otherwise experienced as a city boy. He learned to build things, like tree houses, and in the summers, he and Merle would spend a week roughing it at a scout camp in the woods. They lived in a tent and cooked their own meals, in addition to learning wilderness skills that earned them merit badges.

When he really got into it, Scouting became more than just a casual hobby for Stanley. His ambitious streak and his desire for achievement soon showed themselves, and the ideas of learning skills and earning badges appealed to him.

Over a few years, he earned so many merit badges that he lost count of them. He mastered civics (citizenship), first aid, fitness, bird study and surveying—which meant that he could find his way through the woods using only a map and compass.

He worked hard, and he kept moving up the ladder, earning the titles of Star Scout and Life Scout along the way. Then, he faced the top rung: the rank of Eagle Scout.

To earn it, he had to get what was called a "lifesaving" merit badge, which would show that he could indeed save someone's life in an emergency situation. The summer he was supposed to do this, however, he found out that the camp he attended also had a baseball team.

Now, Stanley was in love with the game of baseball, and he had his Uncle Dave to thank for that. They often went to Pittsburgh Pirates games together, and Stanley enjoyed sitting in the bleachers with Dave's gambling buddies—guys with names like One Eyed Moe.

It cost 25 cents to sit in the bleachers and take in a game in the 1920s—that seems unbelievably cheap now, but back then, even such spare change was sometimes hard to come by. The Great Depression hit America when Stanley was in high school, making every penny count for his family and most others like them.

So, he tried to earn a few dollars by working at the baseball games. He got a job as a vendor, selling soft drinks in the stands. It wasn't long, though, before he realized that it just wasn't the right job for him: he was too big a fan of the sport. Instead of hawking his wares, he would actually stop and watch the games, which didn't make him any money at all.

Well, needless to say, he joined the team at the Boy Scout Camp, to the exclusion of pretty much everything else. And when it came time to be tested for the lifesaving merit badge, Stanley failed.

"I know I could have qualified if I had practiced," he recalled. "I just didn't practice, so I didn't make it."

Disappointed in himself, Stanley accepted that he fell short because of his own behavior, but he picked himself up and moved on. He next set his sights on a special wilderness survival badge, because he wanted to become a member of the Order of the Arrow—an achievement outside the normal ranks, above and beyond Eagle Scout.

In order to earn that badge, he had to sleep in the wilderness, away from everybody and everything for an entire night. Though he doesn't remember much about the experience now, Stanley does have a pretty solid recollection of a lot of darkness and absolute terror.

"I was scared to death," he said. "Boy, was I glad to see the sun rise."

That may have been what brought his dreams of being a forester to a crashing halt. Clearly, his love of nature had its limits. He was proud of making it through the overnight test, but there were more trials he'd have to endure to be admitted to the Order of the Arrow, and he'd had enough.

Unlike the missed opportunity to make Eagle Scout, Stanley didn't regret falling short this time, because he at least tried, and simply found out that it wasn't for him. As long as he did his best, he wasn't one for self-recrimination or regret. When his best wasn't enough, he simply moved on to something that he could better achieve.

His brother Merle did make the Order of the Arrow, but it never occurred to Stanley to be envious. Rather, he was proud of his brother's achievements; throughout his life, he's always cheered others on, even those who were against him in competition or attained things that he wanted for himself.

Stanley remained a scout through high school, and eventually became an assistant scoutmaster. Today he credits his leadership skills and his passion for helping others to those years, noting that they had a lot to do with developing his character. He also learned a lot about integrity, and the value of setting and achieving goals through honest work, ingenuity and determination.

"I have a lot of respect for scouting," he later said of the childhood activity that lay the foundation for a lifetime of merit, spent in pursuit of achievements that, as a young man, he could not yet imagine.

The Hand Brake Story

WHILE UNCLE DAVE WAS RESPONSIBLE for Buddy's love of baseball, Uncle Phil unwittingly introduced him to a slightly more dangerous pastime. Although the family was not able to afford bicycles for Buddy or Merle, the boys did get to play with a set of wheels. When Uncle Phil was promoted to detective the city gave him the use of a Model-T. It was black and shiny, and full of fun levers and wheels and gizmos that caught the eyes of little Buddy and Merle. Uncle Phil often let the boys sit in his amazing car and goof around when it was parked in front of their house. The house sat on one of Pittsburgh's many hills.

Although Buddy now says that Merle was always the more outgoing twin, and the one more likely to pull a prank, at age six it was Buddy who accidentally discovered how to release the brake on Uncle Phil's Model-T. As the car careened down the hill, the screams of little Merle and Buddy pierced the walls of Grandma's house, and floated into the bathroom where their uncle was shaving. When he heard the screams, he ran outside to see what the ruckus was about, his mouth covered in shaving cream. Eighty years later, Buddy still remembers the sight of Uncle Phil, foaming at the mouth like a rabid dog, yelling and chasing after him and his brother as they slid down the hill in the runaway car.

The story of Buddy Pearle might have ended right then, before their uncle could catch them, if the Model T's wheels hadn't turned toward the curb and brought the car to a sudden halt. Still foaming at the mouth, Uncle Phil finally caught up to the boys and bawled them out.

Enter Elsie

DURING HIS TIME AT SCHENLEY HIGH SCHOOL, from 1932 to 1936, Stanley was a star baseball and basketball player. He made good grades and had a lot of friends, but he was a quiet fellow who mostly preferred to enjoy the high school experience from the sidelines.

His twin brother Merle, however, turned out to be an extrovert who joined the most popular clubs, consistently got the highest grades and dated lots of girls. In his typical friendly way, though, Stanley didn't begrudge Merle any of it.

When they were seniors, Merle somehow convinced Stanley to try out for the school play—a farce called *Skidding*. It was a small part, and Stanley wasn't exactly a thespian, but his brother was so enthusiastic about it that he had a hard time saying no. Besides, it was something new, and Stanley was always up for a challenge.

He got the part, and he found himself acting alongside a girl named Elsie Cohen. They'd been in the same circle of friends for a while and he knew her as a pretty, intelligent, vivacious girl. He also knew that she had a boyfriend, though, and besides, he was more interested in sports than girls, anyway.

But they became more friendly over the course of the play,

and they even had some fun together at the school dances that year. Elsie's dance cards, while always full, often had Stanley's name on them.

For their graduation dance, Stanley had planned to take a girl from another school, but his mother suggested that he take someone from his own class. "It's your graduation, after all," she told him.

That made sense to Stanley, so he called the first girl who popped into his head: Elsie Cohen. He knew that she had just broken up with her boyfriend and might actually be in need of a date. He could have asked a lot of other girls—he was well liked around the school and probably could have had his pick—but something told him to ask Elsie, and as usual, he went with his instinct.

Turns out they had a wonderful time at the dance, and decided to go out again—and again and again. Stanley quickly discovered that Elsie was much more than a pretty face. She was a solid person, interested in politics and civic affairs—a real "bright lady," as he described her. He also said that she was attractive, smart and a good cook: "She had everything that most men would want."

Elsie was easy to talk to and it was soon apparent to Stanley that they had a common set of values. They both came from Jewish families of humble means, and they both grew up without fathers—Elsie's had died in a flu epidemic when she was only two.

Although they both came from relatively poor backgrounds, they were optimistic about most things. They'd learned to survive hardship by finding the positive side of every situation, by helping others less fortunate than themselves and by developing the belief that they could always improve their own lot by setting goals and working hard to achieve them. They greatly admired each other.

After high school, Elsie contributed to her family's income

by working as a clerk in a gourmet foods shop in downtown Pittsburgh. Stanley worked nearby at a wholesale jewelry company, and he took Elsie to lunch nearly every day.

They didn't have a lot of money, but they found plenty of ways to spend time together, as young people in love do. Sometimes they went to parties with friends, or to the movies, or just for a walk. They used to go to a popular place near Elsie's house, called Isaly's, which served ice cream in funny, triangular-shaped scoops.

Dating Elsie was more of an undertaking than it seems. Just as he had with the Boy Scouts, Stanley had to travel a long way to woo the girl he believed was the best.

"I had to take several streetcars and walk over a steep hill to get to her house," he explained. Neither of them had a car; Stanley's mother did, and he was allowed to use it, but he always had to fight his brother Lester for it. They didn't get along very well, and they were always in competition it seemed. More often than not, Lester won, and Stanley rarely got to use the car.

So, he wore out plenty of shoe leather courting Elsie. But through all their walks and talks and lunchtime dates, it became clear that they both expected their conversations to continue for the rest of their lives. They knew they were perfect for each other.

But, Stanley didn't want to think about marriage until he was sure he could provide a family with the best possible future. He was a hard-working, ambitious young man, and although he wasn't ashamed of his humble beginnings, he knew that with a little applied determination, he could make a better life than the ones he and Elsie had known.

He knew that he needed to start thinking about a career, and in a roundabout way, Boy Scouting helped him find his way in that department. His old scoutmaster, impressed by the

determination with which Stanley had worked his way
through the scouting ranks, was part owner of a wholesale jewelry company called Grafner Brothers. He offered Stanley a job
as a delivery boy, making $12 a week.

Stanley was happy to have a job—and to be making so
much money.

"People don't realize how difficult it was during the
Depression," he remembered. "People were selling apples on
the street for a nickel. It was a terrible time in American history." He knew that he was lucky to get such a wage. People
were doing anything they could to earn half as much.

Stanley quickly earned the respect of his boss and didn't
remain a delivery boy for long. Even during the Great Depression,
he had what it took to get ahead. He was a fast learner and a
people person who got along well with just about everyone, co-
workers and customers alike.

He was soon a sales assistant and trainee, accompanying
salesmen to other towns to sell goods to jewelry stores. He carried their suitcases, helped take care of the merchandise and
organized their travel plans, all the while watching, learning
and asking questions.

In the Boy Scouts, Stanley had learned the importance of
finding mentors he could respect, following their leads and then
taking the initiative to put their advice into action. They were
simple principles, but they worked. He relied on them with his
new job, and within a few months, he became a salesman.

But, like any achiever, once Stanley reached a goal, he
didn't waste time sitting on his laurels. He didn't want to be a
salesman forever and he kept his eyes open, looking for the
career that would satisfy his ambition, the same ambition that
had won him all those merit badges as a boy.

What might a man do with that much drive? If his family
had money, or if his grades had been more spectacular, he might

have gone immediately to college. Unfortunately, he didn't fall squarely into either of those categories. But as usual, Stanley didn't spend time worrying about what he couldn't do or be. He knew that whatever he chose to do, he had the ambition to take it far, and so he set about exploring his possibilities.

Changing the Course

AS A YOUNG JEWELRY SALESMAN, Stanley met many optometrists; back then, they practiced primarily in jewelry stores, as glasses and monocles were considered accoutrements and accessories.

Ever the friendly person, he got to talking with these doctors during his business visits and learned a little bit about their profession. The more he learned, the more he was convinced that it would be a great way to earn a living—not because of the work itself, but because of the money and the opportunity for dependable employment it provided.

Optometry school was expensive, but Stanley rationalized that at least it was cheaper than all-out medical school—for which he didn't have the grades, money or interest.

"Jewish mothers always wanted their sons to be either doctors or lawyers," he further explained. "That was the custom in those days. So, not being able to consider medical school, optometry was at least something in that direction. It was a close second or third."

After looking into his options, the choice came down to the Northern Illinois College of Optometry in Chicago, or a school in nearby Philadelphia. Once again, Stanley decided that he was willing to travel the longer distance, because he believed it would benefit him in the long run— the Chicago school offered a program that would allow him to attend class year round, and finish in three years instead of four.

As it was, though, Stanley was nervous about how he was going to pay his way through. Such things were certainly cheaper in those days, but to him it was a whole lot of money—especially since he didn't have any to speak of.

To make things even harder, when Stanley tried to resign from his job, his boss offered to increase his salary to $25 a week if he stayed. He believed that Stanley should stay in the jewelry business, and that was a lot of money in 1937—a very tempting offer.

Not one to be rash, Stanley gave the proposition some serious thought. After all, he did want to marry Elsie and start a family, and $25 a week would be a good start. But his instincts told him that pursuing an independent profession would be better for his long-term future, even though he might be giving up a lot of money in the here-and-now.

Even at the young age of 19, Stanley believed it was important to trust his instincts. So, the next day he returned to his boss and told him firmly, "I'm still going to optometry school."

Giving up the prospect of money was tough, but not as tough as leaving Elsie behind. She had to remain in Pittsburgh with her family, whom she helped support, while Stanley went off to school—for three long years. It was a hard time for the young couple. They had been spending all their spare time together, and being apart for that long would be a serious test of their love and commitment.

Working his way through optometry school in the 1930s would not only be a test of Stanley's relationship with Elsie, but a test of his stamina as well. Decent paying jobs were already scarce because of the Depression, and finding a job that would allow him to take classes during the day was even more of a challenge.

During his first couple of years at school, Stanley worked as a night clerk at a small Chicago hotel, six days a week for

$60 a month plus a free room. He'd go to school from about 8:00 in the morning until noon, and then take the 'L' train to the hotel. He'd sleep for three or four hours, and then he'd head downstairs for the night shift.

Stanley worked the front desk from 6:00 at night until 6:00 the following morning—12 long, sleepy hours of watching the door, helping guests and answering the switchboard. He got in a lot of good studying during that time, and occasionally he could convince the bellman to keep an eye on things while he snuck away for another nap.

The guests were a motley assortment: people just passing through, traveling salesmen, full-time residents and even a few call girls. They didn't ply their trade at the hotel, but they lived there. Ever a gentleman, Stanley was always courteous and respectful to them as well as their boyfriends and husbands, who he discreetly covered for sometimes while they stepped out with other women. Shortly after the girls returned from their nighttime jobs and headed upstairs to sleep, Stanley would head out for another morning at school.

During his three years in Chicago, Elsie was only able to visit Stanley a couple of times. She couldn't afford the train, so she had to tag along with Lester and his mother when they drove out there.

During their first visit, Stanley put them all up at his hotel. They arrived on a Friday and had to leave again on Sunday, so that Elsie would be back for work the next day. With the time so brief, and Stanley's family around, there was little opportunity for romance.

During the long year that dragged out between visits, he and Elsie constantly wrote letters to each other.

"At that time," Stanley remembered, "we knew we were serious with each other. We were talking about marriage."

Going South

WHEN HE GRADUATED FROM OPTOMETRY SCHOOL in late 1939, he was eager to get back to Elsie, and to start working in Pittsburgh. But first he had to take a three-day state licensing exam in Philadelphia—and then wait two months to receive the results.

There was also a rumor that because of state board politics, anyone who graduated from the Chicago school would not get licensed in Pennsylvania. This turned out to be false, but the idea, on top of everything else, made Stanley antsy.

He didn't want to sit around and wait for his future to come to him, so in his usual ambitious fashion, he tried exploring some other options. He learned from a school friend that Texas offered a three-day exam, but they would tell you the next day if you passed or not.

Stanley was immediately sold. He raised $100 for the trip and with nothing more than a suitcase, he boarded a train for Fort Worth. It was quite a daring move, at a time when cross-country travel was not very common. His family thought he was crazy, going to live in the wilderness with the cowboys.

"My brothers used to say that I was the one with the adventurous spirit and the guts," Stanley recalled. "But I was very ambitious, and I think that's what motivated me. Coming to Texas turned out to be one of the most important decisions in my life, there's no question about that."

He did pass the Texas exam, and, in almost the same moment, found a place to practice his trade: an optical shop in San Antonio. It was owned by an optometrist's widow, who hadn't been able to make heads or tails of the place since her husband died, so Stanley stepped in and helped run it for a few months.

The opportunity gave him the start he was looking for, while giving the widow some much-needed help. It also gave him a good amount of money, as she paid him $25 a week—the same amount his jewelry store boss in Pittsburgh had offered him three years earlier, before he'd left for school.

While working in San Antonio, Stanley found out that he had passed the Pennsylvania exam, but he decided to stay in Texas. Although he missed Elsie and his family, he sensed that his future was in that frontier land of forward-looking optimism. He strove to make himself a part of his new community.

Stanley made his first foray into the world of mentoring in San Antonio, where he became involved with a Boy Scout troop. He had always strongly believed in public service, and scouting was a natural place to start for him—it had set him on a positive path when he was a kid, and he wanted to give something back in recognition of that fact.

But he was only in San Antonio for a few months before he found a more promising position at a jewelry store in Dallas. Optometrists were in demand then, and jewelry store owners and department store managers were looking for people to set up optical departments in their stores. As Stanley found out, it wasn't too hard to get a job once he had his license.

The job offered $65 a week, a respectable sum in 1940. That money not only represented Stanley's first blush of success, it meant that he and Elsie could finally afford to start their life together.

Shortly after Stanley set up shop in Dallas, Elsie began making plans to move to Texas so they could marry. It wasn't exactly what they'd planned during their three years of waiting—they'd always expected to settle in Pittsburgh, and now she would have to leave her beloved family behind—but she was excited nonetheless.

They exchanged several letters about their plans, though Stanley never formally proposed to Elsie. He told her he loved her often enough; he just wasn't the sentimental type, he figured.

They did talk about their mothers a great deal, though. It seemed that both women were upset about losing their children to such a faraway state. There were tearful goodbyes when Elsie left Pennsylvania, even though both families tried to make it festive by throwing rice at her as she boarded the train for the 30-hour journey to Dallas.

After she arrived, they were married the next day: September 10, 1940. The ceremony was held at the home of the owner of the jewelry shop where Stanley worked. It was a simple ceremony among people they barely knew, but Elsie never looked more beautiful in her smart suit, and the couple were more than happy to be joined together finally, after so many years of writing letters and waiting.

Aside from her wedding ring, there's one other accessory Elsie started wearing after she got married, something she'd long owned but kept secret from Stanley: eyeglasses.

"Elsie was very myopic," Stanley explained, "but she never wore her glasses in front of me. She was very secretive about that. When I found out how near-sighted she was, I was amazed that she could see without them. She must have learned to interpret blurs, because when she looked at a distance she couldn't see. Here's an optometrist, and I never knew she wore glasses until we were married."

Elsie also added a new accessory to Stanley's life—a few extra pounds. After three years of living on his own and working his way through optometry school, his six-foot tall frame was a skinny 160 pounds.

"The first year of our marriage, I went from 160 to 200," he said. "Elsie loved to cook. She'd make delicious food and pies. I remember she made this wonderful pineapple upside down cake."

But Elsie was much more than an old-fashioned home-maker. It was often said in those days that behind every great man was a great woman, but in Stanley's case, Elsie never stood behind him—she stood right by his side all the way.

"She was a real partner in every way," Stanley reminisced. "A lover and a partner. And there wasn't any move that I made without knowing her opinion."

Stanley's practice quickly grew, not only because of Elsie's support and advice, or because optometrists were harder to come by back then, but because patients responded to him. Everyone did.

"I was a people person, a friendly person. And I always wanted to do the right thing. I wasn't a *great* optometrist, but I was *good* one and I had concern for my patients and tried to do a good job."

Stanley had always been hardworking, but he credited Elsie with adding yet another dimension to his life that he'd never much considered before: "I was never sensitive to the beauties of life. But she was, and she opened windows for me. Even though she never went to college, she read a lot and knew more than many graduates. She opened my eyes and made me realize that there was so much more to life than simply making a living. She gave me an appreciation of philosophy and music and the arts, to be able to walk down any street and see the beauty in everything, instead of just the street and the cars. I'm very grateful for that."

Waiting

STANLEY AND HIS NEW BRIDE had precious little time to enjoy those beauties of life, however, before some of the world's ugliness intruded. On December 7, 1941, the Japanese attacked Pearl Harbor, officially bringing the United States into World War II.

In early 1942, they discovered Elsie was pregnant. They were thrilled at the prospect of having a child, but the timing was terrible. Stanley was only 23, and they both lived in fear of the day he might be called to serve his country.

Both their families were worried as well; they all feared that if Stanley was drafted into the military, Elsie might be left alone with a new baby. So, the young couple packed up and moved back to Pittsburgh, where Stanley took over the private practice of an optometrist who had joined the service.

For the Pearles, 1942 was all about waiting. They nervously waited for a draft notice while they happily waited for the arrival of their first child.

When Elsie finally went into labor, she suffered complications. It was a very difficult labor, and the doctor let it go on for an inordinately long time. It seemed that he had seen a similar case before hers, and in that one he had lost the child, so he was afraid to give Elsie anything to make it easier for her.

"In those days, men didn't attend births," Stanley later recalled, "so I was just pacing up and down, swearing."

Elsie came through it all right, and so did their new baby boy, David. But Stanley was shaken by the experience. "It bothered me so much how difficult it was for Elsie. I said, 'No more children.' We'd had enough."

But both of them soon forgot the ordeal in light of the joy their adorable, sweet-natured new son brought to their lives, and just a year later, Elsie was pregnant again. Their daughter Linda was born in 1944, and then the other shoe dropped.

Stanley was drafted.

His brother Merle had already been pulled into World War II early on, in 1942. Merle was assigned to the Air Corps and was initially part of the experimental Glider Corps program. When it was cancelled, he became a regular pilot and flight instructor in Dallas until he was shipped to North Africa. There, he flew missions along the supply line leading to China, ferrying supplies to be used in the fight against the Japanese.

Stanley's military career was not quite as distinguished.

At first, he hadn't been called to service because he had a child. But in 1944, the need for manpower continued, and he was recruited by the Navy.

After completing boot camp, he was told to report for duty as a destroyer tender in Portsmouth, Virginia. The ship was being repaired in preparation to set out for Pearl Harbor.

Miserable over the prospect of leaving his family for a place so far away, Stanley tried to get a transfer to the naval hospital in Portsmouth. He figured that if he got work there as an optometrist, he could bring his family down while he served out his time in the Navy.

"One day," he recounted, "I got a pass and went to the big naval hospital in Portsmouth. I went into the optical department and they were busy. The optometrist was examining people. There were a dozen people and he was overloaded. I was just a midshipman or something like that, but I said, 'Look buddy, I guess you need some help here. I'm an optometrist.' He grabbed me and took me over to the personnel department and tried to get me transferred off the ship. But he couldn't do it because of all the red tape, even though it was clear that they could have used me there. So I went back to the ship and sailed for Pearl Harbor."

It took nearly two months to get from the north Atlantic coast to the South Pacific, via the Panama Canal. That was the longest journey Stanley had taken in his life, his first time at sea and his first time passing through the Panama Canal.

He had MP duty during the passage through the canal. While he was on duty, he heard shots fired, but he and the other MPs ran in the opposite direction. They knew that the commotion meant some kind of barroom brawl, and the last thing they wanted was to get involved in that.

Other than the gunfire, the voyage left little impression on

Stanley, because all he could think about were the wife and two children he'd left behind. When he got out to sea, he was sitting in his cabin and he overheard one of the other fellows singing a popular song, "Sentimental Journey." He decided then and there that he hated that song. He was going overseas and his family was staying behind—there was nothing sentimental about that.

It was a terrible time for those who remained behind as well. Elsie rented rooms for herself and the children at a house in Pittsburgh, near her family. The war was already drawing to a close and Stanley had told her he had little fear he'd see any action, but she was incredibly lonely. They were a very close couple, and it was tough for Elsie to be left alone with two children at what should have been the happiest time of their young lives together.

Baby Linda lived most of her first year without her father, and Elsie was thankful that the young girl probably didn't even know what she was missing. At two years old, David's understanding of why his dad had left was not much better.

"David was very young and we had become very close," Stanley said. "He had heard I was in Pearl Harbor, so when people asked him his name, he replied, 'My name is David Lee Pearl Harbor.'"

Young David also missed the family car, which they had to sell when Stanley entered the Navy. Every time he saw an automobile, David would say, "That's our car."

Alone and miserable, Stanley didn't even have the comfort of being able to serve his country with his most useful skills. He was assigned to the optical department of the destroyer tender, and though it may sound like the perfect job for an optometrist, he knew little about that kind of optics.

"The job of a destroyer tender was to repair damage to destroyers," he explained. "Our department's job was to repair binoculars and telescopes. I was lost. I didn't know one end from the other. I would fool around with them a little bit and learn a little bit about them, but it wasn't what I wanted to do."

Stanley never stopped trying to get off that ship.

Once it docked in Pearl Harbor, there was a beautiful hospital ship that came and lined up next to it. Stanley tried to get transferred to that ship, to do work in their optometry or ophthalmology department, but he was still held back by red tape. All of this served to make him even more disappointed in his naval career, because he felt that he wasn't being used efficiently. His talents were just being wasted.

But it wasn't all bad. He was, after all, stationed in the tropical paradise of Hawaii, and sometimes there was shore leave. On days off, he would go to Waikiki beach; he'd send Elsie pictures of him relaxing in the sun while she was home with two kids. It used to drive her crazy.

In late 1945, Stanley's ship began the long voyage to San Francisco Bay, where the crew could be discharged. Stanley was almost home free, but a funny thing happened on the way.

In spite of his upbringing with an uncle who had a penchant for it—or perhaps because he had been raised to be a better man—Stanley had never liked gambling. But there was nothing like the boredom of several days of rolling across the endless Pacific, combined with the anxious, high spirits of heading home, to encourage a man to do things that are completely out of character.

Stanley got into a card game onboard, and by the time the ship arrived in San Francisco, he had lost his entire paycheck.

Penniless and embarrassed, Stanley asked Elsie to wire him some money.

"Isn't that awful?" he said, sheepish about it to this day. "She hardly had any money."

After she sent him enough funds to make it home, it took Stanley several days amid the bustle of hundreds of sailors to catch a train back to Pittsburgh. Like something out of a movie, one day he just walked up and knocked on the door of his own house; Elsie answered, and she almost fell over when she saw her beloved husband standing there.

As much as they had hated to be separated, Elsie and Stanley were aware how lucky they were. Stanley's military career, while not entirely exciting, was at least short. He never saw action, and after a long year and a half away from his family, he came home in one piece, unlike many others.

"That was the worst thing about war," Stanley said. "Fathers didn't come home and the wives and kids suffered. I'm very grateful that I was not badly affected because I came home and I wasn't gone that long."

Chapter 2

Building a Business

FROM THE MOMENT STANLEY WAS REUNITED with his family in Pittsburgh, he began making plans to head back to the legendary frontier of Texas, the land of opportunity. When he found out that a jewelry store in Corpus Christi was looking for an optometrist, his brother-in-law helped him find a used Chevy for $200. He piled the family in and headed southwest across the country's burgeoning highways.

David was only three, and Linda was one year old when they made that trip. David loved cars, and insisted on sitting up front.

The old car ran beautifully until they were about halfway to Texas. Then suddenly, while they were riding along the highway at about 50 miles an hour, the engine died. Stanley thought, *Oh boy, trouble*, and began wondering how they were going to make it the rest of the way.

Then he looked down and saw David squirming on the seat, and then he noticed, the car's ignition key turned the wrong way. Apparently the little boy who loved cars couldn't resist playing with it.

Stanley and Elsie shared a laugh as Stanley turned the key the right way, and the engine turned over. He drove the old Chevy the rest of the way to Corpus Christi, while Elsie kept an eye on David's little fingers.

Setting Up Shop

DR. PEARLE SETTLED IN AT THE JEWELRY STORE, which was called Lester's, and his practice prospered. He worked, he earned a decent salary and he tried to make up for the time he lost with his family while he was away at war.

His life was stable at that point, and some men might have been satisfied to raise a happy, healthy family on the income from a small, thriving practice. But Stanley wasn't that type of man. He always had bigger ideas cooking on the back burner.

Before the war, a friend named Ted Shanbaum had asked Stanley to become his partner in a new business, and the idea had stuck in his mind all that time. Wouldn't it be great, he sometimes thought, to be your own boss? To do things the way you wanted to—the *right* way?

Ted was an attorney from Chicago who had learned something about the optical business from his brother-in-law and had the idea to create a chain of retail optical shops, independent of any jewelry store or other "host environment." The big draw would be a combo package of cheaply priced eye exam and glasses.

The only thing Ted was missing to complete his plan back then was an optometrist, and that was why he'd called his old friend Stanley.

But at first, Stanley was determined to maintain his independence—in fact, he'd been thinking about opening his own store. He figured that he had a license, and had just about as much capital as Ted did, so what did he need a partner for? He was pretty sure that he could do it himself and not have to worry about the potential burden of a partner. He respectfully declined Ted's offer.

So, Ted instead got together with an optometrist named Ellis Carp and opened a retail business in Dallas, which they called Lee Optical. The company thrived, even throughout the war; while Stanley was away fiddling with telescopes and binoculars in Pearl Harbor, Lee Optical was expanding. By the time Stanley returned to Texas, Lee had around a dozen shops throughout the state.

Later, when Stanley started working in Corpus Christi, Shanbaum started calling him again. He was looking for another partner to help with expansion, and he still wanted Stanley to join him.

And again, Stanley refused. He was still set on opening his own business and doing things his way. But by 1948—three years and many, many phone calls from Ted Shanbaum later—he finally gave in. He hadn't saved as much startup money as he had hoped he would, and he realized that Lee Optical could help him with financing. They could get him out of the jewelry store and set him up in a nice little optical office that would essentially be his own.

Once he signed on with Ted and his company, Stanley became a 50 percent partner in a freestanding business that operated under the name Dr. Stanley Pearle. It combined a medical practice with a retail shop—offering an optometrist on site, as well as optical services and products.

No longer dependent upon a jewelry store host, Stanley enjoyed the freedom his new practice offered, and he dove headfirst into his work, even more vigorously than before. His store prospered, and Shanbaum and Carp certainly noticed.

They liked his style—he was a hands-on owner who was familiar with every aspect of his business and took a genuine interest in not only his patients but his employees as well. His dedication was apparent, and it earned him a lot of praise from both colleagues and consumers alike.

Eventually, Ted asked Stanley to take on the responsibility of running more Lee Optical stores, but in a greater capacity than merely performing eye exams and prescribing lenses. In time, he eased away from working directly with patients, turning his sights more toward developing new stores and finding qualified people to run them. The humble optometrist was quickly becoming a successful businessman.

The owners of Lee Optical wanted Stanley to help them develop all their stores in south Texas, including Brownsville, Laredo, San Antonio, Corpus Christi and McAllen. They made him a junior partner and he got right to work, setting up the goals for each store and knocking them down one by one through hard work, enthusiasm and dedication.

While developing and implementing the plans for each new shop, Stanley learned a lot about the challenges of managing a multi-unit organization. From the ins and outs of hiring employees to training a good management team to keeping tabs on the many financial considerations, he gained some incredibly valuable experience, as well as a good idea of what it was like to truly *own* something.

The greatest lesson he learned, though—from Ted Shanbaum himself—was to "think big," to be fearless in his planning and go for the best, not just what was easiest. He found that when he released his business mind from limitations—when he stopped thinking that his grand ideas were unrealistic and that they could never be done—he was worlds more productive. And what he produced was a better store, a better product and better service for his customers.

Stanley began spending an increasing amount of time in Dallas, where Lee had its headquarters. In 1952, he moved there to play an even greater role in running the company. By then, Lee Optical was growing exponentially—a fact that Stanley attributed mostly to their low prices.

Lee had more than 100 stores and had expanded outside Texas to a few other states, including Louisiana and Arizona. They were no longer operating only out of independent offices, but had also leased departments at jewelry stores such as Zales and Gordon's Jewelers.

No longer directly involved with patients, Stanley instead focused on what he saw as one of the most important aspects of Lee Optical's successful business: good employees. He worked hard to ensure that every time he opened a new store, it was run by people who cared about quality service as much as he did. He hired them, he trained them and he trained them to train other employees well—thus enforcing a cycle of excellent service that he knew was one of the major keys to consumer satisfaction.

But surprisingly, it was on that point that he and Ted Shanbaum had a parting of opinions. To Ted, price was king: nothing came above or before the almighty dollar, and his main concern was how his company (and thus he) could earn more of them. He really seemed to believe that if he simply offered prices that were slightly lower than his competitors, the customers would come running.

To Stanley, on the other hand, while low prices were certainly important, they meant little when they were the *only* "feature" offered. He believed that customers were smart, and that they wanted quality products and professional service as much as they wanted a good financial value.

Price, quality and service: that was the tripod Stanley believed would support long-term success in any business. He worried that Lee was ultimately doomed if it continued to hop along on the single leg of price alone.

"Shanbaum didn't understand marketing," Stanley later said, when looking back on his days with Lee Optical. "If you're going to grow, you have to provide quality service and products. And if you think you're kidding people, you're wrong. I used to have a sign in my office that said, 'The public is smarter than you think.' Don't think that you can fool the public. In the long run, you're going to get hurt. I still believe that to this day."

But that wasn't the end of Stanley's growing criticisms of the way Ted did business. He didn't care much for the way Ted dealt with his employees, either.

"He didn't understand how to handle people," Stanley remembered. "He used the fear technique to scare people into doing what he wanted." Needless to say, this was a far cry from Stanley's personable, humanitarian approach to hiring and retaining quality employees.

There were other minor problems along the way—what business partners don't have disagreements once in a while? But as time wore on, Stanley's disillusionment with Lee Optical continued to grow. He never said it was a bad business—after all, it provided him a good income that helped him support his family well. And there were so many things about his job that he liked. He just always knew, somewhere in the back of his mind, that he could do it better, if only he had the chance.

Learning From the Competition

LEE WAS NOT THE MOST SUCCESSFUL OPTICAL RETAILER in Texas. In those days, Texas State Optical was the area's true eye care giant. Stanley, though loyal to the company that employed him, knew that Texas State was undoubtedly the finest organization in the country.

But instead of hating them—they were the competition, after all, and boy did they give Lee a run for their money sometimes—Stanley admired them. Instead of wasting his energy on grumbling with envy over their success, he spent his time observing what they did and learning from them.

Texas State, Stanley saw, had started out with low prices as their selling point—just as Lee Optical had. But as consumer trends began to veer more toward higher quality and better service, Texas State met the demand. Their marketing strategy was to have the best doctors and personnel, and the best quality frames. They moved away from pricing as their primary focus and they became much more successful than Lee.

Texas State Optical operated almost exclusively in—you guessed it—Texas. They held about a 50 percent share of the market in Houston, which meant that they were responsible for one out of every two pairs of glasses the city's denizens wore. They also boasted a 40 percent market share in Dallas, and similarly large shares throughout the state.

Stanley tried to explain the significance of those numbers to Ted Shanbaum, but his words fell on deaf ears. They had disagreements about the way Lee was being marketed, with Stanley always trying to convince Ted that Texas State's strategy was the way to go. People were grading up, he tried to reason; they were demanding more quality and service.

Ted, though, was dismissive of Stanley's ideas, even though he wasn't proposing anything revolutionary.

"We don't have to reinvent the wheel," Stanley told him. "We have a successful company right here. All we have to do is exactly what Texas State is doing. They're a great company. Let's just follow their example."

When Ted brushed Stanley off with the excuse that Texas State was not Lee's competition—and therefore, they didn't have to approach the business the same way—that was the last straw.

That was when Stanley said to himself, *I have to get away from this guy.* He couldn't believe that Ted could look at a company with a 50 percent share of the market and think they weren't competition!

Shanbaum may have taught him to "think big," but Stanley was ready to think bigger—and he was ready to do it on his own. He had long held the idea of starting his own optical business, and he figured that then was as good a time as any to strike out and just do it.

But, trying to get out of his partnership with Ted Shanbaum and stay in one piece was not easy. Since they had been friends and enthusiastic associates in the beginning, their partnership wasn't clearly spelled out on paper. There were no set provisions to cover what would happen if one of them wanted to leave the business behind.

It took Stanley a year to negotiate a way out of Lee Optical, and from the experience, he learned one of the hardest business lessons there is, the one that is almost always learned in hindsight: always get things in writing.

The settlement they reached was not entirely in Stanley's favor; he was only able to hang onto a few of the assets that he'd earned in the company. He took a substantial loss, but he wasn't willing to put himself or his family through a protracted legal battle that could have taken two years or more.

After spending 10 years building Lee Optical—in 1958, the year he turned 40—Stanley walked away with 15 profitable jewelry store optical departments, mostly in Louisiana. He also got enough cash to make his dream of becoming an independent businessman come a little closer to reality.

He continued to run the few practices he'd salvaged from his partnership with Lee, and bided his time while he built up some capital, all the while looking forward to finally getting to do things the way he wanted. In his usual optimistic way, he wondered if what he got was really that bad after all.

A Culture of Friendly Service

EVEN BEFORE HE STARTED HIS OWN BUSINESS—before he had the real estate, the employees or even a company name— Stanley Pearle knew how he was going to run the place. It was all, he figured, about being friendly.

This idea was years in the making, stretching way back to his days as Buddy, the affable kid from Pittsburgh. Since then he'd spent a lifetime building up the admirable personal qualities that he was now ready to put into business practice: competitiveness learned from playing sports; compassion for those less fortunate; integrity and humility in the face of hardship; selfless generosity; honesty and an utter lack of pretense. With Stanley Pearle, what you saw was what you got, and it would be the same with any company he founded.

He also knew, even as a kid, the truth of the saying, "You can catch more flies with honey than with vinegar," and as he got older, he saw just how it applied to almost every aspect of life. From family to friends to customers, Stanley always knew that the key to keeping people happy was a smile and a little extra attention when they needed it.

With that in mind, he formulated a business model that he called a "culture of friendly service." It was a complete package sort of approach that would present customers with quality products, excellent prices and yes, *friendly service*. This meant having employees who were more than knowledgeable about their business and their products, and who would take the time to genuinely get to know their who would also be their eye care patients.

But he knew, too, that a company couldn't simply

announce that personal service was its aim and expect fantastic results. Establishing a culture of friendly service required a tremendous, ongoing effort.

"You don't get it automatically," he explained. "You really have to work at it and know that's what your aim is. When a person comes to work, you have to tell them, 'This is what we want you to do, this is the way you answer the telephone' and so on."

Stanley believed that it would be worth the effort and attention to detail, even if it cost additional time and money, because people in general were willing to pay extra for personal attention, and because satisfied customers would become loyal customers. It was a simple formula, but one that some business owners missed because they only looked at the straight math, forgetting that the bottom line could be affected by customers' feelings and attitudes about a company.

Stanley recognized that the "customer is always right" philosophy had to be based on much more than big grins and lip service. He understood that if he wanted to build an operation that would grow, he needed to offer something that customers wanted. He knew that he needed good ideas, but emphasized that they were only a beginning. "One of my beliefs is that ideas are a dime a dozen," he explained. "It's execution that counts. You can have an idea but if you don't execute it, it doesn't mean anything."

He also believed that successful companies were dedicated to making personal service a top priority.

"If you go to a place where they get to know you, they call you, and if they promise you something they deliver it, that's the mark of a company that cares about quality and service," he said. "That's when the customers start talking about that company as though, 'Hey, they're friends of ours.'"

Respecting customers was another big issue. "Don't ever look down upon consumers," Stanley advised, bringing up the idea that had driven a wedge between himself and Ted Shanbaum not too long before. "Consumers are smart as hell and they're getting smarter all the time. Be sure that you pay attention and don't try to fool them. That's a big mistake a lot of people make."

Stanley was in fact one of the first in the optical business to recognize that customers were becoming too educated to be lured by low prices alone, and he wanted to further that trend by offering something more. Though they didn't want to pay a lot, they wanted quality, and Stanley was going to give it to them.

A New Vision

STANLEY'S DREAM WAS TO OWN SOMETHING BIGGER than Lee Optical, with greater ambition and more heart. He envisioned a national network of optical stores offering one-stop total eye care in friendly, attractive, professional environments.

In 1961, he opened his first fully independent optical center in Savannah, Georgia. He had carefully selected the place to launch his dream, deciding on Georgia because there was less competition there. There was no Texas State, no Lee Optical, and Stanley thought it would be a good place for his business to grow.

"I didn't want to be a hero," he remarked, "but I wanted to be smart, so I went where there was the least amount of resistance. I went to an easier market."

The new store was a combined optometry practice and eyewear shop, and he called it Pearle Optical—not for lack of creativity, but because he wanted a name that people would recognize and remember, something that reminded them of the person behind the operation, something that would grow from being a simple last name into a popular, well-regarded brand.

By simple definition, a "brand" is a name (usually trademarked) that identifies a business or a product. Back then, when Pearle Optical was just starting out, "branding" was not the huge business unto itself that it is today; Stanley didn't have studies and statistics to rely on when choosing a moniker for his company.

But by putting his own name up there on his first store, he sure was onto something, whether he knew it at the time or not.

The concept of a brand has more subtle connotations than just the name itself. It has to do with name recognition—and what emotions and qualities consumers relate to it.

Stanley understood this concept when he said, "For our business, we wanted a name that people would think of when they thought about glasses. We wanted people to say, 'Gee, that's a company I've heard some good things about, and some of our friends went there and liked it.'"

It was a simple concept from back in the days before mega-conglomerates ruled the corporate world, before every business decision was studied and planned down to the minutest detail.

But Stanley had a clear vision on this subject and, if nothing else, he was sure of one thing: people would have confidence in the Pearle Optical brand because they knew it was founded by a professional optometrist with enough faith to put his name right out there on the front of the store.

Stanley's first store had a modern-looking façade with a striped awning, and an attractive window display advertising glasses for as low as $12.50—an excellent price for the time.

But what counted most to Stanley was not the good-looking veneer—it was everything else behind it that really mattered.

Back at Home

WHILE STANLEY WAS BUSY PLANNING THE BUSINESS of his dreams, at home he and Elsie were building the family of their dreams. It was almost as if they started two families, 10 years apart: after having David and Linda in 1942 and 1944, Gary and Roberta were born in 1952 and 1954.

No matter how many there were in the Pearle family, there was always a clear message that they were all in it together.

When Stanley broke away from Lee Optical, he and Elsie called a family meeting to explain what was going on. They told the children that they would be budgeting a little more, that Dad would be traveling a little more and that Mom might be working a bit more.

These sacrifices paid off. Soon the Pearles could afford to send Gary and Roberta to private schools, and all of the children were assured the opportunity of the higher education their parents could never afford for themselves.

But success also had its drawbacks. Stanley had started traveling more frequently when he worked for Lee, and when he started his own company, he was gone almost every week. It was hard on the family. He came home every weekend, but his wife and kids missed him.

Stanley tried to take a philosophical view on the matter.

"There's no question that we did suffer a little," he said. "I think, as I look back, that I missed some things with the children. But on the other hand, we gained a lot, too. There are always things in your life that you might have done a little better. But we had a close family, and still do, and I don't have any real regrets."

Stanley was often out of town on business, but it was a time in America when dads were expected to spend most of their time outside the home, earning the daily bread, and weren't expected to take a large role in family life. By that standard, he was more involved than many fathers and did his best to maintain close-knit family ties.

He would send the children letters from the road and bring little gifts for them when he returned. When he was home, he made extra efforts to attend all of the children's school plays and games.

He even managed to take the entire family with him on several business trips. His daughter Linda laughed when she recalled the way her dad always tried to impart his own positive attitude to the rest of them, trying to make them see the bright side of everything.

"Sometimes these trips would be cancelled at the last minute," she said. "We would be packed and ready, and he would find out the morning before that he was not required to go. We'd be disappointed, but my dad would say, 'What are you so upset about? You had all the fun of the planning, the packing and looking forward to the trip. You already had half the fun of traveling.'"

Being the oldest, and being exceptionally close to his father, David was perhaps in the best position out of all the children to observe his father at work. Stanley often brought David along on car trips. They bonded easily over a mutual love of sports, particularly baseball. Stanley often went to David's baseball games, and in turn, David went to his father's softball games.

Stanley, the star high school athlete, never really left sports behind. David recalled, "When I was a kid growing up, Dad used to play in traveling softball leagues. They were good teams and he was a good player."

Later, the pair also played tennis together. David said that in sports, as in business, his father always exhibited the character of a winner.

"Even though I became a more talented player, he would often win. He just had a great athletic temperament. He was competitive, but knew how to keep his poise under pressure. He was always great in a clutch."

Roberta was always impressed by her father's positive attitude.

"I found it amazing, given his history. Although he didn't always have the best role models, I think he was able to pick the best of his early experiences and bring the best of himself to everything."

Linda said that he'd always been a man of integrity, and he tried to instill the same value in his children. "Growing up, Dad always held us to a very high standard. Any kind of fibbing or lying was not tolerated."

Their father's honesty went beyond simply telling the truth. He shunned any kind of mask or pretense, and insisted on always being himself. As Gary put it, "He's wonderfully unselfconscious, what you see is what you get. I would give anything to be as comfortable as he is with other people. He's sort of a model in that way."

While their father's honesty, generosity and friendliness would have made him a good role model by action alone, he was also fond of telling his children basic aphorisms to live by. Roberta said, "He kind of boiled life down to simple sayings that sounded kind of hokey and corny. He used to say, 'I don't care what kind of grades you make, as long as you do your best.' And when we got together as a family one of his favorite sayings was, 'These are life's precious moments.'" She paused to laugh. "It sounded kind of corny, but now that I'm older I realize he was right."

He also made sure his children understood the value of hard work, and he taught them never to act as if the world owed them anything they had not earned. "As a teenager, I worked at his office," Linda recalled. "And whenever someone was going to the post office, or to get lunch, or to run errands, my dad said, 'Linda will do it.' I complained, 'Why do I get all the grunt work?' And he said, 'Because everyone else here earned their positions. You're only here because you're my daughter.'"

Setting aside all the aphorisms, Stanley boiled down the most important lesson he taught his children to one word:

integrity. He always felt that is was the most important thing in life—just to be honorable and decent. That's the thing he tried to teach his children.

All four children recalled that their parents were extremely close, even though they were opposites in many ways. Their eldest son David described his parents in short: "My mother was sort of a Bohemian intellectual and a live wire. My father was one of nature's gentlemen, a strong, silent athlete type."

Elsie was a progressive woman for her time. "She was probably a Socialist in high school—it was pretty common back then," David said. "She was also very artistic; she had magnificent taste in art. She did community theatre when we were in Corpus Christi. That was a little bone of contention between them, because he got jealous—she was so pretty, you see. But she was also extremely bright. In today's world, she would be a doctor or lawyer."

Roberta recalled, "Dad and Mom had a traditional division of labor, but he was very modern in that he had tremendous respect for her. He really believed marriage needed to be on even ground."

In the early years, Elsie helped Stanley with his business. But even then, she was the one who kept the home fires burning. And oh, what a fire she burned! All of the children remembered that their mother was a fabulous cook. She even wrote a cookbook, along with their rabbi's wife, a Frenchwoman.

"Mom was good at cooking everything," Linda said, "including the Jewish types of foods: matzo balls, strudel, gefilte fish. Those were pretty much Passover foods—I think that was everyone's favorite holiday."

Cooking was just one aspect of Elsie's creative talents. She also entertained with great flair, whether it was an event for business or charity, or a gathering for family and friends. David recalled, "My mother just entertained in such an elegant way. She was like a born artist. Everybody wanted to come."

Their home was open to many, but family was foremost. Every Friday night the family celebrated the Jewish Sabbath with a big dinner, often surrounded by plenty of extended family and friends. The children were never allowed to go on dates on that night.

Stanley remembered those nights with fondness. "Elsie was a religious person. Friday night was important. We lit candles and said prayers. All the Jewish holidays were always big events—Passover and our fast day, which was Yom Kippur. We enjoyed celebrating all of the Jewish holidays."

"My parents came together in very consistent and reliable ways," Gary says. "Passover was always beautiful and there was always room for a large number of people. During all of those holidays and special occasions, our house was a wonderful place to be."

Gary said that both parents encouraged the children to explore their individuality, although this was their mother's special talent. "My mom always said that her own mom always managed to give each of her four children the sense that he or she was her favorite. And she did the same for us. She gave us a deep level of trust and affection. She was a very physical person, very comfortable in her own skin, and able to give you a big hug and really appreciate wherever a little kid was coming from. She had an enormous capacity to appreciate someone for what he or she really was. The role she played in helping us feel self-confident was very important."

Gary thought that that side of Elsie was also a tremendous help to his father. Stanley's own mother had never been as demonstrative with her love. "I doubt he was ever held or hugged much as a child," Gary speculated. "I suspect that being married to someone who was at ease being affectionate in that way probably helped give him a reserve of confidence. That was what my mother gave him behind the scenes. But in his early business life, she worked with him professionally as well."

David put it simply: "They were partners in every sense of the word."

Chapter 3

Vision and Planning

IF YOU WEAR GLASSES OR CONTACTS, your last visit to the optometrist was probably almost as simple and painless as buying a new pair of jeans. You probably didn't have to drive far, you probably went to a place that combined a medical office with a nice place to shop, and there were probably so many frames and lenses to choose from that it took you a while to make up your mind.

Further, the optical shop you visited was likely part of a retail chain, and you might have gone there to take advantage of a deal you saw advertised on TV, or a coupon you cut out of the Sunday newspaper.

These things are so commonplace, you probably don't think about the convenience any more than you think about the ease of running out to the supermarket. But getting an eye exam and purchasing glasses used to be much, much more difficult.

43

When Stanley Pearle started practicing in 1940, eyewear often wasn't a pretty sight. Strong prescriptions usually meant heavy, ugly lenses—the proverbial soda-bottle glasses.

"When I look back at some of the horrible glasses I put on people," Stanley later joked, "I'm almost ashamed of myself."

People who didn't wear thick lenses were still stuck with a limited selection of frame styles—a phrase that was something of an oxymoron, as most frames were not stylish, but ranged from nondescript to downright ugly. The best option was to look for the least objectionable pair. Needless to say, back then people only wore glasses if they absolutely had to.

In 1940, most optometrists still offered their services in private practices or inside department or jewelry stores. A visit to the eye doctor was often viewed as a dreaded medical appointment, not an opportunity to go shopping.

And there were no coupons or special deals. Many optometrists did not even advertise, because they considered the idea of competition in a medical field unprofessional.

In those days, most optometrists contracted out for lab services. This meant that they would perform the exams, but then send the prescriptions to another place to be turned into glasses—which involved a lot of people and a lot of time. That's just one reason glasses were so expensive.

Those who didn't have the patience or money simply skipped the exam and went straight to the five-and-dime to buy their reading glasses, which meant that they were not always getting the right prescriptions for their eyesight deficiencies.

For those who did go through the whole professional optometry route, there weren't a lot of frames to choose from, either. Unattractive glasses were the bane of many a school kid, and even more so to adults on the dating scene. Taunts like "four eyes!" and sayings like "Men don't make passes at girls who wear glasses" were enough to make people avoid wearing the eyewear they needed.

But Stanley Pearle aimed to change all that. He was ready to create a new business based on the marketing strategy he'd learned from watching Texas State Optical, the practical management skills he'd learned while working for Lee, and his own unique blend of friendliness, integrity and dedication to service.

He also aimed to make going to the eye doctor a more pleasurable experience. For too long, he felt, optometrists had been getting a bad rap; their patients seemed to hate them, and for Stanley, that just wouldn't do. He knew that all it would take were a few little tweaks to drastically change people's attitudes toward caring for their own eyes.

Stanley's business model was simple: convenient locations, expanded hours, professional exams, friendly service and a large selection of quality frames at competitive prices. At first, he would focus on the pricing to draw customers in, but then he would gradually increase the emphasis on the other quality products and services the company could offer.

In short, his goal was to make going to the eye doctor less like a dreary medical appointment and more like an exciting shopping trip. A tall order, to be sure, but Stanley had been trained to think big.

His vision was to open a chain of optical centers, spread across the country, that would change the way America bought eyewear. He wanted to pull the optical business out of jewelry shops and department stores and put it into separate establishments with identities of their own.

In this new kind of operation, there would be an optometrist either in the same building as the dispensary, or right next door. These optical centers would be attractive places to shop, with larger selections of eyewear than most people had ever seen before. And at a time when the costs of other health-care services were rising, these stores would actually be able to offer lower prices in the optical field.

Stanley made the marriage of lower prices and bigger profits possible by making the most of a simple fact in the optometric profession. The secret of his success relied upon a simple bell curve: he figured out that 75 percent of all prescriptions landed right in the middle of the spectrum. This meant that, while there were some extreme cases that required specially made lenses, for the most part, average people needed just a few repeating prescription types.

Once he knew this, it was easy for Stanley to see what he could do to make the process of filling an eyewear prescription faster and more convenient. To start with, he could inventory those most-used lenses in the stores' cutting and edging labs, to fill the most common prescriptions.

Then, all a lab technician had to do was put each lens into an edging machine and trim it to fit whichever frame the customer selected. In this way, they could fill prescriptions quickly, because they wouldn't have to grind the lenses. It meant that the stores could service 75 percent of their customers' prescriptions right on the spot, making the speed of delivery faster than it had ever been before.

Expansion

THOSE WHO HAVE MET STANLEY PEARLE believed that his company simply reflected the characteristics of its founder—a point that he has humbly conceded.

"That fellow at Lee Optical, Ted Shanbaum, believed in fear, in scaring people. It's just the opposite of me," Stanley said. "I didn't believe in fear at all. Shanbaum lost a lot of wonderful people by chasing them away. That's why his company ultimately failed. I, on the other hand, was able to attract really good people and keep them. That's why we grew."

And grow Pearle Optical did. It seemed that Stanley's choice of the path of least resistance, so to speak—his settlement in the previously optometry-challenged state of Georgia—had paid off. Profits at his one shop were so good that others soon sprouted up like dandelions across the state.

By 1963, just two years after he opened the first store in Savannah—which became known as Pearle-1—he christened Pearle-47. Unbelievable though it seems, Stanley had a hand in each and every one of them, too. He personally passed on his culture of friendly service at each new store, reminding every employee that their purpose was to help the company grow by giving customers what they wanted.

To finance their continuing expansion, that year the company went public, under the name Opticks, Incorporated—after a term used by Sir Isaac Newton, which Elsie had noticed while perusing a bookstore. They raised more than $600,000 through the sale of 74,000 shares of common stock to 1,000 shareholders.

The chain's profits were consistently good, which caused their stock prices to go up; by 1964, those initial shares were valued at about $1.8 million. A secondary issue—in which Pearle Optical sold off another portion of its business—accumulated even more wealth for the company, and for its owner. Stanley and Elsie Pearle, both products of working class America and the Great Depression, were well on their way to becoming millionaires.

"I'd never seen that kind of money before," Stanley remembered. "When I worked at Lee, I never saw any, never had any personal financial assets—just a home, a car and things like that. This was the first time I had some capital to do extra things."

As most good business owners do, when Stanley first made money he put a lot of it right back into the company. But Pearle Optical's rapid expansion soon allowed him to spend a little bit on himself, too—and his family.

As he had longed to do for quite a while, he finally found

the resources to become more involved in charity and political causes; Elsie was able to collect more of the artwork that she loved; and they were both able to give more to their children than they'd ever imagined they could.

Although Stanley had always been ambitious, at that time in his life he looked back on the humble aspirations he had in the beginning, and he laughed.

"When I was in optometry school, a friend of mine and I were talking about our goals," he recalled. "And he asked me, 'If you could settle now to make $50 a week for the rest of your life, would you be happy?' I said yes, because $50 a week was a tremendous amount of money back then. Over the years, I've often looked back on that and said to myself, 'My God! I would have settled for that, and look what's happened!'"

By 1966, Opticks, Inc. owned more than 100 Pearle Optical shops, officially making it the new giant in the U.S. eye care field.

All of that expansion meant that Stanley had to become something of an expert in another field: real estate. Location, he quickly found out, was a key element in his successful business. Since part of his original plan was to offer convenient, one-stop eye care shopping, he put a great deal of thought into where each new store would live.

In the beginning, he did a lot of real estate scouting himself, along with his Georgia supervisor, Dr. McClintick. They would go into a town together, talk to real estate agents and try to get the best sites they could find. They wanted the downtown stores that were right in the middle of everything, the ones with the most traffic passing by. They'd try to find a location on the busiest block of each town's main street—but if that weren't available, they'd sometimes settle for the second-busiest block.

But Stanley also tried to approach the location issue with

some outside-the-box thinking when he could. He knew that where his stores were physically placed was important, but sometimes the ideal spot was too expensive. So, he set his mind on finding innovative ways to open shops in the most desirable areas.

One of his most ingenious ideas was to buy abandoned gas stations and convert them into Pearle Optical stores. Many of these establishments were going out of business in the 1970s because of the nationwide gasoline shortage. Stanley noticed that the empty structures were almost always located favorably, on busy corners with good parking—perfect high-traffic locales for his growing optical operation.

During just one year in that decade, Pearle opened up 100 stores, at the rate of two a week. Each had an opening budget of $25,000, in addition to its regular budget. At that time, Pearle also spent $60 to $70 million a year for advertising.

As Pearle Optical grew, finding these special locations became a full-time job, and Stanley and Dr. McClintick hired real estate developers to do the scouting for them. In later years, they found that the best locations were in shopping centers—purveyors of one-stop convenience at its finest.

Doing Something Big

IT WAS OBVIOUS BY THAT POINT THAT STANLEY PEARLE had hit on something with his new brand of retail-friendly optometry, but he was characteristically humble about his reputation as an innovator. He always insisted that the model in his mind was his old competitor, Texas State Optical. He believed in emulating those who were successful, and improving on their models wherever possible.

But whether he realized it or not, he was much smarter than he took credit for. Texas State's greatest flaw, perhaps, was that its owners were only interested in Texas. They didn't think big.

Stanley's ambition was to go national.

For such an undertaking, he realized that he needed to bring more than just his own unique talents to the table. So, just as he meticulously interviewed and hired employees for his stores, he set about carefully choosing a partner for his new venture, and he settled on his old friend Bill Benedict as the best possible choice.

Bill was a longtime leader in the optical lab business in Dallas, and he had recently started his own laboratory. Shortly after Stanley had broken away from Lee Optical, he'd turned to Bill to supply him with lenses and lab services. They got along so well that Stanley suggested they merge their companies and "do something big."

That something ended up being a partnership that incorporated both Bill's new lab and Stanley's new network of eye care centers—a combination that had previously been unheard of. The benefits of the pairing were completely new as well—by partnering with a lab owner, Stanley created vertical integration between supplier and retailer. This increased efficiency and cut costs, which meant that their customers could enjoy lower prices while Bill and Stanley received greater profits.

But profits without principles were out of the question for Dr. Pearle. When he and Bill drew up the contract for their partnership, he warned the attorneys that there would be "no slanting, no choosing sides." He asserted that he and Bill were partners, and that everything had to be fair between them. It was the way he had always lived, and the way that he would run any business he was in charge of.

But even though he was a fair man, Stanley was no pushover—which became apparent to Bill the day they went into a bank to ask for a business loan. While the banker—a friend of Stanley's—hemmed and hawed and told them a dozen reasons why they shouldn't go into business together,

Stanley sat calmly and listened. When his friend was done, he simply asked, "So are we going to get the money or not?"

Bill was impressed with Stanley's straight shooting attitude, and as they began to work together he became privy to Stanley's true advantage in the corporate world: he was fair and kind, but he was also an unexpectedly tough businessman. He saw this again and again throughout their working relationship.

"One time," Bill later remembered, "we were in New York, negotiating to buy 16 new stores. We made what we thought was a fair offer. The other side jumped up and put their coats on. They said, 'You're too far off. There's no point.' So I picked my coat up. But Dr. Pearle chuckled and said, 'Bill, wait a minute. They'll be back.' And he was right. A few minutes later, they came back. He knew we'd made a fair offer."

Stanley always insisted that for a deal to be good, it had to be good for both parties. When it came to his partnership with Bill Benedict, he knew it was a beneficial arrangement for both of them. Stanley ran the retail end of the business and Bill ran the lab, and together they were very successful. They helped each other grow—as one part expanded, so did the other.

As the company grew, Bill's lab attracted business from independent optometry practices all over the country, in addition to the work he did for the Pearle stores. This brought a lot of extra money into the company, and it was an innovative move that Texas State Optical had surely never attempted.

But how were they able to handle all the extra work? The lab had originally been intended to serve only the Pearle Optical stores. So what was the secret to doubling, sometimes even tripling the lab's ability to produce quality products?

Simply, they turned it into a wholesale operation. They found that by using mass production techniques, they were able to fill a tremendous quantity of prescriptions for their own stores, as well as for doctors and opticians around the country, at greatly reduced costs. And their products never suffered any reduction in quality.

It was definitely a new concept in the field of optometry, and it certainly sealed Stanley's reputation as an innovator. Up until that time, most laboratories were very small and could only do small amounts of work, usually for high prices.

But after the evolution of automation and mass production methods, the same labs could be capable of offering many, many doctors the same supplies they were used to, but at almost 50 percent off the cost. This was exactly what Pearle did, and the response was just phenomenal.

When Stanley and Bill built a new lab in Dallas in the early 1970s, it was one of the largest in the country. It covered 120,000 square feet and employed 250 people just to fill prescriptions. It was busy from the day it opened, and it's still in operation today.

Bill Benedict has said the phenomenal success of their new company was due greatly to his relationship with Dr. Pearle. "The real key always had to do with the partners involved. We were together for about 10 years, and it was a remarkable relationship. We never had one disagreement. I think it was Dr. Pearle's personality, his own giving way."

The right partner was just the beginning. Dr. Pearle knew it was also important to attract highly qualified optometrists. So, when he selected an executive to oversee his Georgia operations, he chose a fellow optometrist: Dr. Charles McClintick, who went by the nickname "Chili."

"He was a wonderful man from my Lee Optical days who followed me to my new company," Stanley explained. "He'd been a commanding officer in the Air Force and he was a great leader. I based him in Atlanta to help with the development of Pearle in Georgia and the beginning of the Pearle system.

Later, Dr. Jack Sham joined us, another excellent optometrist, to help oversee operations in the Midwest. I was fortunate to be able to attract some very great people, because that's one of the secrets of growing. You have to attract and keep good people, and you have to take care of them properly."

Dr. Pearle believed that since he, Chili and Dr. Sham were optometrists, they were able to attract other highly qualified professionals from the same field more easily than other companies.

"It was important to attract the best doctors we could," he noted, "because there was a lot of resistance in those days to our type of practice. Independent optometrists were trying to discourage their colleagues from working for large companies because they thought of them as too commercial. But I convinced our optometrists that they could practice good optometry in a so-called 'commercial environment.' I told them, 'Come in and practice good optometry, because unless you do that, you're not going to grow anyway.'"

From Personal Values to Business Ethics

TO STANLEY PEARLE, THE BOTTOM LINE for a successful business was not much different from the recipe for a successful marriage: common values, mutual respect, an openness to new ideas and a desire to grow.

Dave Pierson, former president of Cole National, said on the occasion of Stanley's 80th birthday that "Dr. Pearle has brought integrity to this industry, brought stability to this industry and brought fun to this industry."

Longtime Pearle optometrist Dr. Howard Oifer took that praise a step farther. He gave his mentor credit for more or less *creating* their industry, at least in the form that it exists today.

"I really believe that he changed optometry," said Dr. Oifer. "He created the basic format on which the optical business is run today—having a doctor on premises, a lab in the store and a large selection of frames. No matter where you go to for optical care today, they all have the same basic set of features, and a professionally trained staff. I'm still operating on his format, 25 years later."

Whether in public life or private, it was Dr. Pearle's sense of values that left the strongest impression on those who knew him.

"The most important thing that Dr. Pearle always talked about was being ethical and being honest," said Dr. Oifer. "He always told me that you can't separate being an ethical person from being a successful businessman. He said that he never saw someone who was unethical in business and a good person outside of it. He said that you could never be successful unless you were honest, trustworthy and did the right thing."

Dr. Phillip Wolf also considered Stanley a role model of ethics in action. "He was really a model of probity and complete integrity. Some people got to high status by ways that were not always clean, but I don't think you could ever say that about Stanley. It's important to him to have a good name, and that means a lot. You can be ruthless and super-successful financially and be detested. It's an important Jewish value to have valor, to be a person of value. With Stanley, that's a ringing characteristic."

Dr. Pearle's nephew Chuck Cohen was an attorney for Pearle during a time when the company was growing by leaps and bounds, and making some important mergers and acquisitions. During many high-stakes meetings, he saw that his uncle had a knack for creating the kind of positive energy that made things happen.

"He was such a straight shooter, such a good guy, that everyone always liked him and trusted him, and therefore he could make these business deals work. There are many opportunities in business, but unless a person has the strength of personality to make them work, they're not going to become realities."

Integrity, honesty, ethics, good guy, straight shooter: those are the kinds of words people used to talk about Dr. Pearle's character. And those are the kinds of words Dr. Pearle used to talk about the kind of character he believed *everyone* should have.

"In business, you have to deliver what you say you're doing, and you can't be deceptive about it. I think it's important in your personal life, too. People can spot a phony," he said.

While Stanley believed that integrity was a foundation for good business, he understood that it was *only* a foundation. Somebody once asked him what it took to be successful in business, and his answer was, "The secret to success is finding a business where you're going to do well even if you make a bunch of mistakes."

He also believed that there was an element of luck in success, but others believed that his personality gave him a special knack for picking up on ideas that other people missed—and for being ready to spot luck when it arrived.

William Yost, who became Pearle's chief legal officer and secretary, thought that special knack was critical to Dr. Pearle's success. "I remember one day I was giving him a ride to the Milwaukee airport. Everybody else always took him on the expressway, but I took him on the scenic drive along the shore of Lake Michigan. And he looked around and said, 'This is a beautiful city. I've never seen this before.' He has always had the ability to see things as if they're brand new. He lives in the moment.

"There's a childlike quality that I think characterizes a lot of creative people. If you could characterize business as a creative occupation, you could certainly do it in his case. That would be how I would describe Stanley: creative, and able to look at the world with new eyes. That means you're looking at things differently than the other guy, who's carrying a lot of baggage. One thing Stanley didn't do was carry a lot of baggage.

Because of that, he found a way to change the paradigm in his field."

When it came to managing people, Dr. Pearle based his approach on principles that have long existed, though not all companies have had the courage to follow them. He not only believed in surrounding himself with smart, talented, honest people; the next step was trusting, respecting and relying on them as well.

When he was looking for new ideas, he believed in asking for, and seriously considering, plenty of input from those who worked for him.

"At a meeting he would sit and go, 'Mmm-hmm, mmm-hmm,' and you could see the wheels were turning, and then *bang*, you'd have an answer," remembered Mr. Yost. "Stanley was not one of these people who tended to shove a meeting around, or ride close herd. He tried to draw people out and get them to think creatively. He was not a pushy manager."

Dr. Pearle said that in management, "It's important to give responsibility with authority." By giving qualified people his trust and confidence, then staying out of their way and allowing them to perform, he empowered those who worked for him to put their unique talents to work and come up with dynamic results. That approach also instilled a sense of loyalty throughout his company.

He sometimes lamented of other business leaders, "Very often people give responsibility *without* authority. Then they wonder what happened." He believed that if a manager gave someone responsibility, then interfered in their decisions, it could create an atmosphere of fear and mistrust in which people felt too stifled to perform at their best.

But he pointed out that giving someone responsibility with authority also meant asking that person to accept responsibility for the results.

"You have to make accountability the next thing you look for," he said. "You have to see if the person is performing. If he's not, you have to be strong enough to make a change. That can be tough. Some people are afraid to make a change when they're not satisfied with performance, and that's not good."

By "make a change," he meant anything from changing a policy to firing an individual.

No matter how successful a company was, Dr. Pearle advised friends and associates that it was never time to sit on their laurels. As Dr. Oifer said, "The main thing he taught me was to be open to new things. He always said, 'Don't start believing your own publicity and think you know everything. That's when you get into trouble.'"

Dr. Oifer described Dr. Pearle as a very flexible man, both in his openness to new ideas and in his dealings with others. On the other hand, he said that Dr. Pearle's values were unwavering, and his sense of honesty, fairness and compassion applied equally to all.

"He had certain principles he always followed," Oifer said. "He admired his competitors. He rarely ever had a bad thing to say about his competitors. He was always such a classy human being and always found the best in everybody."

Longtime friend Dr. Phillip Wolf said, "He had a combination of self-assurance and modesty. He never bragged about what he'd done or what he'd given."

Even though Dr. Pearle was the founder of what was at the time the biggest company in optometry, Dr. Oifer found him to be "always down to earth. He was always approachable, always willing to help somebody, always a man of his word and a man of integrity."

When Dr. Oifer was preparing to graduate, Dr. Pearle suggested he go to Georgia to set up a practice with Pearle. The young man immediately accepted the offer, and started work at his first store in Roswell, Georgia, in September 1980.

Dr. Pearle not only understood the importance of finding good people like Dr. Oifer, he knew how to hang onto them. He made it a priority to give them support and the sense that they were valued.

Dr. Oifer remembered that Dr. Pearle made use of networking before it became a popular business term. "When I started out in practice, Dr. Pearle would always send me to other doctors in the Atlanta area. He would tell them, 'My friend Howard is coming to you. I want you to help him, I want you to tell him what you know.' He would tell me, 'Howard, this guy is really on the ball, you could really learn something from this person. Go see him.' It could be anybody. If he met someone who had new ideas about how to market things, or who had new equipment or new techniques, he would send me to them. And he would always follow up to see if I actually did it. He was always calling me about things he saw or learned in his travels, and sending me articles that he thought were pertinent to my practice. And he was always concerned about how I was doing, how my family was doing."

Dr. Pearle tried to instill Dr. Oifer with the same principles that he lived by, teaching his protégé to hire the best people and pay good salaries. He frequently visited Dr. Oifer's store and never left without giving him an evaluation of what he thought the optometrist was doing well, and what he needed to improve.

"He'd write it all on a piece of paper, fold it up, stick it in my pocket and say, 'Here's what you need to do, son.' I almost always implemented his suggestions. He never had an ego."

One way Dr. Pearle has continued to infuse the business he founded with his personal values and philosophies is through the ongoing leadership of people he has mentored along the way—people like Dr. Oifer. In later years, when Pearle was acquired by another company, Dr. Pearle convinced the new parent to hire Dr. Oifer as a consultant in professional affairs.

Oifer remained a consultant for almost two years, traveling around the country to advise other Pearle optometrists about marketing and to teach them how to run their practices.

Dr. Oifer repaid Dr. Pearle's generosity of leadership and friendship with tremendous loyalty. He has remained with the company for the past 25 years. He started as a leasing optometrist, but within two years, he bought the store. He's remained a franchisee since 1982, and is now the largest Pearle franchisee in the United States, with 10 locations in the Atlanta area. After 25 years, he still owns and practices optometry at the Roswell store. "I've been in the same spot, with the same hours, since 1980."

Because Dr. Pearle genuinely cared about all the friends and followers he'd gathered throughout the company over the years, he was able to wrap them all into something more than a company: he developed a community. Without ever setting foot in a business school, taking a sociology class or studying a psychology book, Dr. Pearle instinctively grasped the simple concept that people did not feel loyalty toward the impersonal concept of a company, but toward other people.

He always had a knack for inspiring loyalty, friendship and dedication by simply giving that same loyalty, friendship and dedication to others.

"When Dr. Pearle shook your hand and gave you his word, it was golden," said Dr. Oifer. "He would always do what he said, and that's rare in a competitive profession like his."

Dr. Jeff Smith, a former associate vice president at Pearle, never reported directly to Dr. Pearle, but he, too, considered the founder an important mentor. He first met Stanley when he was working as a part-time on-call optometrist in the Pearle system, while he worked on his MBA.

Like Dr. Oifer, Dr. Smith first met his boss in a roomful of people, at a regional business meeting in Chicago.

"That was the first time I saw how well he was received," Dr. Smith reported. "I mean this in the best way, but I often thought he should be in politics, because there's that knack politicians have of working a room. It wasn't any particular thing he said. He simply recognized each person as an individual. He had an instinct for making each person feel that he appreciated his or her unique contribution, and he could accomplish that in a very short time. By the time he left the room, he'd made everyone feel good."

Dr. Smith said that he'd learned much from watching Dr. Pearle deal with people, and that it helped him tremendously in business. But he believed that few people have the innate talent for people that Dr. Pearle had. He was always especially impressed with the way Dr. Pearle balanced his respect for people's individuality with his talent for bringing people together to work toward a common goal.

"Franchisees tend to be independent in their thinking," Dr. Smith pointed out. "And it was amazing to me that when he went to a franchise meeting, he had that knack for galvanizing a group. He made them realize that they could have individual ideas, but that we still had to pull in one direction."

Dr. Smith thought that part of Dr. Pearle's ability to create a rapport with everyone he met came from working his way through every rung of the socio-economic ladder, from growing up in a working class neighborhood during the Great Depression to starting his first optometry practice, to becoming the owner of America's first nationwide optical company.

"He had personally walked so many strata of the socioeconomic ladder that he could identify with everyone," Dr. Smith said, "no matter what rung they were on, and he had compassion for all of them."

Dr. Smith said that Dr. Pearle had always expressed concern for others in his business dealings, down to the smallest details. "I remember when the company headquarters used to be down in Dallas. When we had meetings and it came time for lunch, many times they'd send me to the McDonald's across the street. I remember that when everyone was giving me their orders, Dr. Pearle would always be real concerned that I wrote down everything accurately, so that everyone had exactly what they wanted—'Now that's a large fry, not a small fry. Now, that's a Diet Coke, right?' I thought it was funny that someone of that stature was so concerned that someone got the right burger. But he just wanted to make sure everyone was taken care of."

One of the most important business lessons Dr. Pearle shared with Dr. Smith was simply to always put the customer first.

"I remember many situations when we were taking about how to improve business and how to improve a region," said Dr. Smith. "He always put in a remark that brought it down to a customer level: what will the customers' reaction be, how will it affect the customers, what will the experience be like for the patient? He knows that's what it comes down to. Where are you going to make the investments? Well, what is the biggest payoff from the patient's point of view? It's really easy to get distracted, but that's a real nice compass—you go back to that point and everything will be okay."

The Advertising Game

THE SPEED OF PEARLE OPTICAL'S SUCCESS was overwhelming, and it was all Stanley could do to ride the tide. He didn't have an MBA, as many other entrepreneurs did, and as he himself said, he was "flying by the seat of his pants" on a lot of decisions.

But what he lacked in formal education, he made up for in business savvy. He studied other well-run companies; he figured out what they did right and wrong and tried to emulate their practices.

One thing he figured out for certain was that good marketing was essential to a company's success. He spent many hours researching the subject—deciding which markets he wanted to cater to, learning what the people in those markets wanted and figuring out how Pearle Optical could give it to them.

Stanley knew that it was of utmost importance to concentrate on the people he knew he could reach. With that theory in mind, he relied heavily on advertising, which was at the time a very new development in the field of optometry. He didn't let that stop him, though. Stanley was not afraid to advertise his business aggressively, emphasizing price, value and the easy availability of professional services.

Because there were as yet no other nationwide optical retailers, Pearle was the only one with coast-to-coast advertising campaigns. This gave them a clear advantage over the local competition in every market the company entered.

As you might expect, those local doctors didn't like Pearle very much. Many private practice optometrists claimed that patients couldn't trust eye care companies that advertised, and that sentiment is understandable. Some of them had been the only game in town for years, and then all of a sudden, in came a big chain optical store that took away half of their business. Why would any of them say anything *good* about a company like that?

So Pearle Optical had its work cut out for it. Stanley knew that they would have to try twice as hard in some places to win consumers' trust, because to him, that was what optometry was all about. When patients went to get eye exams and buy glasses, they were putting the care of their vision into the doctors' hands—trusting these professionals with one of the five senses that allowed them to lead normal, productive lives.

Stanley recognized this bond, and he'd felt it for many years with every single one of his own patients, right from the time he had starting practicing as an optometrist. But now, as the head of a large company, how could he possibly make customers believe that he—and thus every person who worked underneath him—was trustworthy enough to take on this enormous responsibility?

Because he couldn't do this on a personal level like the local optometrists—it just wasn't physically possible to be in every Pearle store on a regular basis—he knew that advertising would play an important role in winning the hearts of eye care consumers across the country. It would be an important method by which he could get his company's name out there, and make it a brand that everyone wanted to be a part of.

To some extent, Stanley was uncomfortable with the idea of commercializing his business in this way. He knew that price had to come into the picture at some point—it was the most obviously marketable feature of Pearle Optical—but he was diligent about not letting that take the focus off of their customer-centered policies. Mr. and Mrs. Middle America, he believed, wanted to do business with someone who would really take good care of them, not just give them a cheap deal.

From that idea came one of the company's most memorable slogans—the 1980s' "Nobody cares for eyes more than Pearle," a jingle that many Americans can still hum from memory today. The slogan was meant to help people feel more comfortable with the idea of going to a retailer for eye care, and it must have worked, because early in that decade Pearle became the largest network of optical outlets in the world.

Chapter 4

Competition

As Pearle Optical grew up to become Pearle Vision, the company's rapid rise to fame and fortune was not without obstacles. Perhaps one of the most difficult to overcome was the ever-present hostility of many smaller, independent optometrists.

Many in private practice did not appreciate or respect the concept of corporate-run optometry; they thought that by putting the focus on making money, the chain-store doctors were demeaning their profession and not giving their patients the care and attention they needed. Some were concerned that motivated by profit, larger companies would put pressure on their optometrists to meet sales quotas by prescribing lenses to and pushing services on people who didn't need them.

Marketing, advertising, one-stop optical shopping—all of it was repulsive in the eyes of most smaller practitioners. Many believed that optometrists who wanted to be of service to others, and who saw optometry as a helping profession, should be content to work like family physicians, in humble, private practices.

According to Stanley, this opposition was one of the biggest problems Pearle Vision faced throughout its many years in business. These attacks, he thought, were inane—the optometrists who worked for corporations were just as qualified as anyone else in the field. The examinations they performed were as good as any private-practice doctor's. The fact that they worked under a trade name didn't make any difference.

In fact, he always ensured that anyone working for him was up on the latest and best advances in the field, so that they could indeed provide the best possible service to their customers. Ironically, this was made possible by the very profits decried by the private operators. Optometrists working for corporations often found it easier to run their practices more efficiently than the independents because they were afforded the best equipment, training and assistance the company's money could buy. Many independents could not do the same, simply because they didn't have the resources.

But the smaller practices tried to discourage their colleagues from joining the larger companies. "Don't work with them," they would say. "All they care about is making money. They don't care about patients." Sometimes they scared good doctors away from working for Pearle. That just made Stanley's job of recruiting the best of the best even harder.

The way he saw it, though, some doctors were good, some were bad, and those who were bad didn't last—at his company or any other. He was sure that many optometrists in private practice were no less motivated by profit than any of the larger companies. Why else would they be working, if not for money? It seemed like a hypocritical stance for many of them to take.

Beyond that, Stanley saw the independents' anti-corporate sentiments as anti-consumer as well. Though they purported to be protecting customers from bad service, he believed what they were really doing was feeding misinformation to the public and limiting the available eye care choices.

The independent optometrists didn't see it this way. They only saw the corporations threatening their way of life. But instead of improving their own businesses, or trying to understand how a chain optical business really worked, many simply chose to go after their competition. And since companies like Pearle were the biggest obstacles their little businesses had ever faced, they had to do something huge to get people's attention.

So, they didn't attack the competition physically, or through malicious advertising campaigns. Instead, they used something much more powerful, perhaps even sinister: the law.

When Dr. Stanley Pearle started his business, many state optometry boards were run primarily by private-practice eye doctors. Aside from approving licenses and overseeing the optical businesses in each state, these boards also had the power to influence governmental regulations within their own field. And, in Texas and many other states, these self-styled independents lobbied for restrictions that made it difficult for large optical retailers to set up shop.

Dr. Pearle had some ideas of his own about his opponents' motives. "The simplest way to defeat your competition," he noted, "is to influence laws that exclude your competition from doing business. And the more lobbying power you have, the easier it is to do that."

Thanks to these independents and their fervor to bring down corporate optometry, eye doctors in Texas—back then, and right up until today—could not work directly for non-optometrists. This meant that they could not be employed by retail optical outfits such as Pearle Vision, because it was a company rather than an individual medical practitioner. The same went for the old standard jewelry and department stores' optometry sections.

The most an optometrist could do, then, if not part of a privately owned practice, was lease space from one of the above-mentioned establishments. And if he had to do that, in some states, he faced a whole other set of regulations.

One regulation required his practice to have a separate entrance from the company's dispensary, where the actual glasses were sold. There had to be a solid wall between the two, and the dispensary was not allowed to make appointments, provide staff or offer business services for the doctor next door. It was as though they each had to pretend that the other did not exist.

Optical companies called this a two-door operation, and needless to say, they were not thrilled about its implications. Having to separate the doctor from the retail business meant adding more doors, walls and furnishings—all of which increased the cost of doing business.

Texas State Optical ran two-door operations for years, and still experienced success. But the extra expenses undoubtedly cut into the company's profits.

When Dr. Pearle was first looking for a place to set up his new business, he firmly did not want to stay in Texas, because he did not agree with all those rules and did not want to have to abide by them. He did some research and found that some other nearby states had rules that were just as bad, if not worse.

He also discovered that since eyewear prices were often higher in states with more regulations, people sometimes drove to states with fewer restrictions to purchase cheaper glasses. That seemed to settle it for Stanley: he had to find a state that would not restrict his soon-to-be booming business.

Back in 1961, Georgia placed relatively few limitations on

the business relationships and activities of optometrists, and that is largely the reason Dr. Pearle began his new endeavor there. Fewer regulations would mean a smoother, less expensive start.

It also meant that his capital would not be diverted toward making extraneous architectural modifications, but instead invested in the business itself. In short, moving to Georgia meant that he could offer lower prices and hopefully attract a lot of customers.

But later on, as his business spread throughout the country, Stanley was not able to escape state boards with unwaveringly strict policies. As Pearle Vision sought to expand, he did have to deal with costly regulations, in Texas and other states.

Ultimately, even Georgia began to pass stricter laws that made running a business there difficult, including rules that prevented optometrists from working for corporations and limited the number of offices an optometrist could own.

Private-practice optometrists saw such regulations as a way to rein in a trend that they claimed could hurt patients. But Dr. Pearle saw the regulations as nothing more than a way to prevent competition—a move that he thought would *truly* hurt patients in the long run, by limiting their choices and driving up eye care costs.

He knew that if he ever had the chance, he would fight those regulations. But, for the time being, they were the law and he had to obey.

So just as Texas State Optical had, Pearle Vision found ways to work within the system. In states that prohibited optical companies from directly hiring optometrists, the company instead leased space to them, a practice that it has continued through today.

In several states, the company also had to deal with two-door operations, where the doctors were completely separate from the dispensaries. These setups did nothing but increase costs and decrease sales. Before long, Stanley was aware that fewer customers were going from the doctors' doors to the dispensaries to get their glasses. Most people, he knew, wanted to purchase eye care and eyewear at the same location.

Most of Pearle's profits traditionally came from the products they sold—not from eye exams—so this one regulation really struck a chord with the company financially. It seemed like a vindictive gesture doled out by the private-practice optometrists, who were the only ones allowed to offer exams and sell products in one location. So, they were getting more business, and Pearle was getting less.

To Stanley, it felt like a personal attack. But, as usual, he simply carried on and made the best of the situation, sure that in the long run his company would prevail.

One thing he always did toward that end was stay on top of the latest trends in the field, even though he was no longer directly practicing optometry; he also made sure everyone who worked for him did the same.

"I kept up with what was going on with the independent optometrists," Dr. Pearle added. "Because if you want to compete with the them, you'd better know how to do it."

Although he believed in advertising and in keeping a close eye on his competitors, he made it his business to avoid mean-spirited tactics. "There's a way to be competitive without being nasty and cutthroat about it," he said, noting that in the field of optometry there was a real problem with organizations stealing each other's people.

"You can't stop them from hiring each other's people—that's legitimate. But there are ways of doing it that are ethical, and ways that are unethical. I always took the ethical approach."

According to Bill Benedict, "I never knew Dr. Pearle to

take advantage of a situation. He's just one of these great human beings. He's an extraordinary person. The book on business says, 'Don't bring your personal feelings through the door.' But Dr. Pearle was not afraid to carry his feelings into the business world."

Luckily for both his employees and his clients, the kind of feelings Dr. Pearle brought into the business world were optimism, gratitude and a great faith in people.

The Personal Cost

THE CONSTANT POLITICAL STRUGGLE with optometrists in private practice not only cost Dr. Pearle's company money over the years—he believed that it affected him personally.

After the war, his brother Merle had followed in his footsteps and gone to optometry school. Around the time Stanley began working with Lee Optical, he coaxed Merle to come to Texas and take the licensing exam.

The brothers, who had been so close throughout their youth, missed each other terribly after several years apart. They were excited at the prospect of living near each other again.

Unfortunately, this dream of theirs was not to be. The Texas Optometry Board gave Merle a failing grade on his exam. Stanley found it impossible to believe his brother had failed on his own merit; Merle had always been the better student and had always performed better on tests. If Stanley had passed, surely Merle would have as well.

In time, Stanley came to believe that the state board treated his brother unfairly, motivated by petty jealousy and fear of competition.

"I have no doubt he passed that exam," he said. "I know they did it deliberately, because they knew he was my brother. They wouldn't let him practice in Texas because they were worried he would be a commercial optometrist, like I was. So they failed him."

Stanley never got over the disappointment, and later regretted that he didn't encourage his brother to sue the board. Merle wasn't the only one this happened to. Stanley believed that the state board tried to keep a lot of potential optometrists out of Texas by failing them on their exams, regardless of their qualifications. He also believes that the same practices still prevail in some states today.

After he was rejected by the Texas board, Merle went back to Pennsylvania, where he handily passed the license exam. For the next 50 years, he practiced in Ebensburg, a small town in the Allegheny Mountains; his office was about an hour outside of Pittsburgh, the city where he and Stanley had grown up.

Ironically, Merle never joined any kind of corporation. Though he may have gone the "commercial" route had he moved to Texas and joined the Pearle Vision team, he always remained in private practice in his home state.

Sadly, the twins who had been so inseparable in their youth spent most of their adult lives many miles apart, although they both would have had it otherwise.

Innovation Through Adversity

DESPITE THE PROBLEMS PEARLE EXPERIENCED because of the smaller practitioners and their control of the state boards, his business continued to flourish. The force of corporate eye care, it seemed, was unstoppable, no matter what the private businesses threw at it.

It seemed obvious to some that it was all a classic case of the little guy hating the big guy. Ironically, Stanley was the little guy once, and through hard work and honest ingenuity, he became the big guy. Whenever a person or a business succeeds in that way, they're bound to get some stones chucked at them once in a while.

Stanley attributed his company's continued success, even through difficult times, to its basic principles. He knew all along that small independents could not provide service as good as his stores offered. They couldn't give their customers as wide a selection as they'd find at Pearle Vision.

In short, Pearle was passing the benefits of their more efficient operation on to consumers in the form of lower prices and faster service. And, at a time when small, one-man operations routinely put huge mark-ups on eyewear, the Pearle difference was obvious to anyone who cared to look.

But Pearle, along with its other retail optical brethren, contributed much more to the world of eye care than customer satisfaction. In fact, they truly contributed to the advancement of some very important innovations within the field of optometry.

Chain stores actually helped to make eyeglasses safer for those who had to wear them. Back when only glass lenses were available, there were many gruesome reports of people whose eyes were gouged by shards when their lenses shattered for no apparent reason. It was later learned that normal wear and tear sometimes put too much stress on the lenses, and they simply exploded.

Because of these events, the federal Food and Drug Administration really dogged the eye care industry, mandating that the glass used for lenses had to be hardened somehow.

The larger retail outfits were the ones who ultimately brought better lenses to the public and made wearing glasses a less hazardous experience. At first, plastic lenses were offered, but when it was discovered that they scratched far too easily, they were replaced with impact-resistant polycarbonate lenses.

Bill Yost, a representative of Pearle Vision since the 1970s, remembered going to Washington to work on the industry's stan-

dards for the hardening of lenses. "I don't see how that innovation could have become the norm without the big companies,"
he said. "They were better able to financially implement the
change."

If You Can't Beat 'Em...

DR. PEARLE SPENT MOST OF HIS CAREER TRYING to prevent the
new industry he'd created from being regulated out of business. He had no choice but to spearhead that battle, because
his company was the first of its kind to do business on a
national scale, and regulations varied—and continue to vary—
from state to state.

To that end, he was eventually able to do what he had
vowed to do from the beginning: change the laws that limited
his business' operations. In later years, the Texas State Board
began admitting members who were not strictly from private
practices, and Stanley managed to get a seat for himself. He
served on the board from 1985 to 1997, and during that time,
he did everything he could to reverse the damage that the
board had already done.

First, he fought to keep the rules in Texas from becoming
any more constricting than they already were. Frustrated by
the fact that the board overlooked real quality of care issues in
favor of simply regulating the forms of the practice, he brought
a different point of view to the table. He even dared to suggest
to other board members that their many rules and "standards"
might actually hurt consumers instead of helping them.

By becoming involved in lobbying efforts, Dr. Pearle successfully countered the historically negative campaigning
against companies such as his own. He also successfully convinced many lawmakers that his type of business was good for
the profession of optometry, and good for the patients it served.

Dr. Pearle also became president of the National Association of Optometrists and Opticians, which was made up of optometrists and executives from the leading optical chains. The NAOO's main purpose was to deal with the many legal problems their profession faced. Member companies were often aggressive competitors in the marketplace, but within the organization, they presented a united front to fight efforts to restrict their business activities.

With the help of the NAOO, Stanley and others in the business went to courts and legislatures and lobbied to open up competition in their field, to benefit their customers. They explained their side in the battle with private practice optometrists, and tried to convince lawmakers not to pass regulations that they believed inhibited competition.

They ultimately succeeded in involving the Federal Trade Commission in the fight.

In the 1970s and '80s, the FTC conducted investigations into regulations of the optometric and optical goods industries, as well as the pros and cons of optical businesses that advertised versus those that didn't. They ultimately found that there was no real difference in quality of service between the two, and that state rules prohibiting vision care providers from advertising were unfair.

The commission also found it unfair that some doctors failed to release eyeglass lens prescriptions to their customers, in effect preventing patients from filling their prescriptions wherever they chose.

So the FTC came up with the Eyeglasses Rule, which prohibited states from banning honest advertising about eye care or optical products. It also required vision care providers to release prescriptions to their patients. The section regarding advertising was later found unnecessary, because it was already covered by a U.S. Supreme Court ruling: in 1977 the Supreme Court ruled that prohibitions on honest advertising by licensed

professionals (including doctors and pharmacists) were uncon-
stitutional, amounting to illegal limits on commercial free
speech.

This was a breakthrough for optical corporations. To this
day, states cannot stop any vision care providers from conducting honest advertising, and the FTC's prescription release rule is
still in effect. The FTC then went on to investigate other common restraints on commercial practices, some of which
prohibited optometrists from: working for or forming business
relationships with non-optometrists; opening practices inside
departments stores, optical stores, shopping malls or other so-
called mercantile locations; owning or operating more than one
office; or practicing under a trade name.

In a rulemaking proceeding known as Eyeglasses II, the
commission did extensive research, held hearings and conducted
surveys. The commission came to the conclusion that many of
the states' regulatory restraints on "commercial" practices were
against the public interest and in fact injured consumers.

After reviewing mountains of testimony and written sub-
missions by thousands of witnesses, as well as conducting its
own exhaustive economic study, the FTC found that many of
the restrictions cost customers more money, decreased the
quality of care available in the market and limited access to
care without providing any offsetting benefits.

In response to these findings, the FTC adopted the
Eyeglasses II Rule. This was actually a set of rules intended to
prevent enforcement of four types of state regulations, namely
those that prevented optometrists from: working with corporations, opening offices in commercial settings, opening
branch offices or using trade names.

This was a victory for Dr. Pearle and his colleagues.
Unfortunately, the victory was short-lived.

The rulings were appealed in federal court by the American

Optometric Association (which represents optometrists, most of whom are in private practice), several state boards of optometry, several of the states themselves and a number of individuals. In 1991, the case made it to the D.C. Circuit Court of Appeals, which ruled against the FTC and vacated the new federal regulations.

The court ruled that the FTC could not pre-empt state laws relating to competition unless Congress specifically gave it that authority—basically, they were saying that the FTC had trampled all over the states' rights. And under the U.S. Constitution, states are not absolutely bound by federal anti-trust laws.

To Stanley, it was a terrible disappointment. But as usual, he went on and did what he had to do to keep his company up, running and on top.

The Lasting Effect

AT THE TURN OF THE NEW CENTURY, the friction between independent and corporate optometrists is not as heated as it used to be. Excellent operations such as Pearle Vision are so good, and the public has responded to them so positively, that the smaller practices no longer have any grounds on which to oppose them. So, although the restrictions are still severe in some places, the arguments are more difficult to sustain.

But many state regulations continue to increase not only the cost of doing business; they also prevent optical companies from offering consistent services from state to state. It can be difficult to run national ad campaigns when the company can't make the same promises in California as it can in Pennsylvania.

It can also be difficult for a national company to grow, or to maintain consistent internal policies, when rules for hiring and for setting up a practice are different in Texas than they are in Maryland.

Today, only 11 states allow retail companies like Pearle
Vision to employ optometrists directly: Illinois, Maryland,
Michigan, Minnesota, Missouri, Nebraska, New York,
Pennsylvania, Utah, Vermont and Wisconsin, as well as the
District of Columbia and Puerto Rico. Of the 39 states that
forbid corporations to employ optometrists, four also forbid
them to even lease space to optometrists: California, Maine,
Delaware and Virginia. To add to the confusion—and the
expense—while California does not allow optometrists to have
any kind of business associations with optical retailers, it *does*
allow them to be employed by a special form of state-licensed,
single-service HMO that provides eye care only. The state also
has similar systems for dentistry and pharmaceutical services.

Several optical companies have secured licenses to run this
type of health maintenance organization. Among them is
Pearle VisionCare, which is owned by the same parent company as Pearle Vision. But the state attorney general is
challenging whether that relationship should be allowed. As it
is, running that type of HMO costs more than a typical Pearle
Vision operation, so the benefit to the company is question-
able anyway.

As Dr. Pearle sees it now, the biggest problem that faces
optometry today is the lack of cooperation between states. If
an optometrist is licensed in one, he or she usually cannot get
licensed in another without going through an entirely new
examination—a double standard that is not true of most other
medical professions.

He believes that not having this reciprocity hurts a lot of
people in the field of optometry. It makes relocating, which is
sometimes necessary due to factors such as a spouse changing
jobs, almost impossible.

Yet, in spite of this obstacle course, Pearle Vision continues
to hold a prominent place in the eye care industry, running on

much the same principles as it did at the beginning. It still offers attractive stores where people can find great service, quality products and professional exams for competitive prices.

Try as they might, the private practice optometrists who opposed Dr. Pearle's type of business never defeated him. In fact, for more than 20 years, Pearle Vision remained the number one optical retail business in the country. The business he founded still thrives today, more than 40 years after the humble opening of Pearle-1 in Savannah.

Chapter 5

Opportunity's Knock

BY THE LATE 1960s, PEARLE VISION had already grown beyond its owner's expectations, but at one point, Dr. Pearle came to a surprising realization: none of his children had an interest in taking over the company when he retired.

"My children never were interested in the optical business," Stanley recalled. "I wish they were. Both of my sons had great business ability. They were tops in math and everything else, but they were not interested in business."

Although Stanley had hoped at least one of them would take an interest in his livelihood, he encouraged them to find their own dreams. "We didn't put pressure on them on what to go into, who to marry, how to live their lives," he said. "We were really fortunate—they were good students, and they didn't get into trouble. They had their own interests, and that was good. It's a great thing for a parent to know that he's given his children an opportunity to do what they want to do. That's important."

In fact, when Gary decided to major in drama at Yale, his parents couldn't have been more proud. "A career in the arts is not necessarily going to be secure financially," Gary later said, "and it doesn't necessarily match what a parent's dream might be. But I always felt as if my dreams, passions and pursuits and my ability to self-direct were important to them. To my parents, raising kids was not about setting achievement agendas, but about helping their children feel loved and important, and they just clearly agreed upon that." In 1977, Gary received a grant from the National Endowment for the Arts to work as a director at the Arena Stage in Washington. It was there that he created an important production of his own, a successful musical called *Tintypes*, together with his future wife, Mary Kyte, a dance choreographer and actress, and composer Mel Marvin.

Stanley still tells people how his son's show became a big hit, and made it to Broadway in 1980. It was nominated for three Tony Awards including best musical, and theatre groups around the country still perform it to this day. Gary went on to direct many plays in New York.

Like Gary, Roberta also developed an affinity for the theatrical arts. She was perhaps the spunkiest of his children, and she remembers now that her father had great reserves of patience for her independent ways.

"He likes to tell this one story about me," she said. "He would say, 'Now, Berta, she used to run away from home when she got mad, which was about every other day.' When I was little, we had a park nearby, and I would run away there. As the youngest of four, I tended to be the most outspoken and demanding, not to be forgotten. I was very colorful, and I don't think he knew what on earth to make of me. But he went with it, he didn't fight it. He didn't make a lot of demands, and he was an easy touch. Actually, I think he sort of liked that we had this relationship where I challenged him a little bit."

Selling Up

SO ALTHOUGH HE WAS PERHAPS JUST A LITTLE BIT disappointed that he would not be passing the company he built on to future generations of his family, Stanley was always one to make the best of circumstances. He decided, in consultation with Bill Benedict, to sell the business.

But lack of familial interest wasn't the only good reason to pass it off to the highest bidder. Interest in acquiring the fast-growing company was high at that time. Several interested companies were jockeying for position, putting Pearle and Benedict at a bargaining advantage.

Finally, in 1968, Dr. Pearle was able to find a buyer that not only made an excellent stock offer, but also wished to leave him in charge of operations, as company CEO and a member of the board of directors. Will Ross Hospital Supply Company, based in Milwaukee, Wisconsin, thus took over as Pearle's first parent company.

The fact that the buyer was already in a medical-related field, Stanley and Bill thought, would help Pearle Vision maintain its image of professional respectability within the health profession. And that, in turn, would help the company further squash criticism from independent optometrists.

"We had a chance to capitalize," Dr. Pearle said. "They paid us a nice price and we still ran the company as if we owned it. We just became part of a larger company. Financially, it was very rewarding."

Pearle Vision continued to grow for the next few years. Profits continued to rise under Stanley's leadership; his instinct for business, which was, as always, based on his instinct for people, never failed. As the public face of the company, his charismatic yet approachable nature still helped to create a positive company atmosphere. His ability to attract the best employees and maintain a loyal customer base was as solid as ever.

When the thriving company changed hands yet again—in 1973, when Will Ross was acquired by G.D. Searle, a pharmaceutical firm based in Chicago—Stanley remained as the president of Pearle Vision. As such, he often interfaced with G.D. Searle's CEO at the time, a man by the name of Donald Rumsfeld. Most now know him as the U.S. secretary of defense under President George W. Bush.

"He made a lot of money for G.D. Searle and he learned a lot about the optical business," Dr. Pearle said of Rumsfeld. "He did a good job, but he was a very tough guy. He cleaned house and he was pretty ruthless."

Rumsfeld was known as the "hatchet man"—he went into Searle's headquarters and basically cut out redundancies that were costing the company a lot of money. For example, there was a human resource department with about 400 employees. He laid many of them off and instead switched to using the HR departments in the company's various subsidiaries.

Harsh tactics, sure, but Pearle Vision was incredibly profitable and grew enormously while under the G.D. Searle's umbrella.

Though he was still very much considered the head of the company, at that time Stanley was becoming less involved in the day-to-day operations of Pearle Vision, focusing primarily on marketing and regulatory affairs. He had brought in a man by the name of Don Phillips to take over as CEO, and he left most of the big decisions to him.

Franchising

DR. PEARLE HAD BROUGHT PHILLIPS ON BOARD as a vice president, but ultimately handed off to him the position of CEO. Phillips was a tough businessman and quickly earned the admiration of Searle's CEO Rumsfeld.

Although Phillips and Dr. Pearle were very different sorts of people, Stanley thought highly of him. "He was very self-centered and he wasn't a people person," he noted, "but he was a very good analyst of businesses. Although Don wasn't outgoing and didn't have the same qualities I had in dealing with people, he had other qualities that were better than mine. He was very good at business marketing and just a good businessman in general."

Under Phillips' direction, Pearle Vision underwent its greatest expansion thus far. Together, he and Stanley came up with a way for the company to grow faster with minimal capital investment: they decided to get in on the trend of franchising. It was the first time any optical company had tried such a thing.

According to Dr. Pearle, "It turned out to be very successful. We could expand faster because it wasn't our money—it was the franchisees' money. And we could attract the kind of people who wanted to be their own bosses, not work for a corporation. They paid us royalties, but they managed their own businesses. In turn, we provided services such as marketing, lab services and other support."

Franchising helped Pearle Vision plug a minor drain on its system. In the past, optometrists with ambitions to become independent entrepreneurs simply left the Pearle chain. But with franchising, more of the people who came onboard stayed onboard.

The new endeavor also helped Pearle Vision in its public relations battle with private practice optometrists. With franchising,

it became more difficult for those optometrists to paint themselves as small, independent medical professionals fighting an
uncaring, Goliath corporation that was out to squash them.

"The idea of doing franchising took some of the curse
away," explained Bill Yost, "because you could say these franchisees were small businessmen themselves."

Not that franchising didn't have its drawbacks. "Sometimes we
had franchises that didn't perform well, and they hurt the brand
because they had a tendency to be independent and to want to do
things their own way," Dr. Pearle said. "So there were plusses and
minuses, but I think the plusses outweighed the minuses."

Franchises also allowed Pearle to take better advantage of its
national advertising campaigns. Television commercials often
reached households in markets with no Pearle Vision offices
available to serve them. With franchising, the company could
quickly jump in and fill that void, going into markets it might
otherwise have taken months or years to enter.

Today, Pearle Vision remains the largest optical company
involved in franchising. About 60 percent of their 790 stores
are franchise operations.

By the early 1980s, the brand was so well known that 8 out
of 10 people surveyed identified Pearle when asked what company came to mind when they thought of eyeglasses. The
business also had the largest network of optical outlets in the
world, with locations in the U.S. and Puerto Rico, Mexico,
Canada, Germany and the Netherlands.

Charity Begins at Home

CLEARLY, DR. PEARLE EMBRACED THIS OLD ADAGE. After years
of traveling and building his business, Stanley wanted to invest
more time and effort in his other interests—his family, of
course, and the other lifelong passion he and his wife Elsie
shared: public service.

He always made an effort to offer encouragement and support to family, friends and colleagues. But his generosity was not limited to those he knew personally.

As his company reached the heights of its success, Stanley never stopped giving tirelessly of his time, money and effort to not just one or two, but many charitable causes. He became one of those successful Americans who believed that success carried social responsibility, and he was determined to fulfill his obligations in that area—and not just for the tax breaks.

Many of the people closest to Dr. Pearle believe his generosity as a friend, mentor and philanthropist was grounded in his humble background. Family friend Dr. Wolf put it this way: "He came from humble origins, and I think he never forgot that. A lot of people came from less than desirable beginnings, and they got to a point where they had clout and some financial success, and they forgot. But he never forgot. Most people who've accumulated wealth tend to be defenders of their own purses. He was the opposite—someone who constantly thought of the disadvantaged and supported them."

Dr. Pearle did not attribute his generosity so much to his humble beginnings as to the humility he felt in the face of everything he'd received since. "I've always felt that I've been so fortunate in my life," he once said. "It sounds corny, but I've always believed that I owed it to society to give something back."

Whatever the reason, from the moment Dr. Pearle had anything extra to give back, he started giving it.

In fact, when he went to work at his first optometry job in San Antonio, he immediately got involved with the Boy Scout troop at the local temple. He was not a scoutmaster, but he did what he could to be a helpful mentor to the boys there.

But he wasn't the only one who was interested in such noble pursuits. After World War II, when the Pearles had moved to Corpus Christi, Elsie struck up a friendship with the wife of a rabbi in the local Jewish Reform Temple. Stanley had not grown up in a deeply religious household, but he'd always felt a connection to his Jewish roots and with Elsie's help, he began to get in touch with his spiritual side.

To Stanley, it was only a quick hop from spiritual to charitable. "If you are religious at all," he explained, "you have to try to help people who need help. I think it's part of every religion, and certainly one of the religious instincts I have is to help the weak. That's Christianity, that's Judaism, that's Islam—help the weak rise up. I believe that when you help the underprivileged or the middle class, then they become strong. I think it makes the country stronger."

Dr. Wolf further said of Dr. Pearle, "He's always been very aware of the world around him, and he's very open in his views."

Elsie was also a great believer in helping others, and she did it with such sincere joy that her generosity drew the admiration of all who knew her. Dr. Wolf recalled, "Elsie was a remarkable lady. She would read three or four books at one time. She knew what was going on in the world, and she was involved with everything. She was a real dynamo, a woman who had an enormous amount of energy and put it to use."

At first, back in the late 1940s and '50s, Elsie and Stanley were primarily involved in organizations relating to the struggles of Jews throughout the world and causes like the new state of Israel.

"I've always been interested in anti-Semitism, which was more prevalent in my younger days," Dr. Pearle explained. "Discrimination was very bad. And of course, my generation lived through the Holocaust. It's still hard to believe that six million people were slaughtered. It was unbelievable to think that people were killed just because of their religion. And some of them weren't even religious. Like most Jews, I think that increased my interest in Jewish causes, as a matter of self-preservation.

"I maintain that no Jew who lived during that time or who knew the history of the Jews could fail to be conscious of the importance of involvement in Jewish causes. The Jews have long been scapegoats for dictators—I'm not just talking about the Holocaust, but things like the deportation of Jews from Spain and the pogroms in Russia. To not be involved, I would think you'd almost have to be asleep, because of our history."

Dr. Pearle saw his involvement in these matters as only natural. He had not only compassion and generosity, but the energy and dedication to turn his good intentions into meaningful actions. He was a member of the Anti-Defamation League and the National Conference of Christians and Jews, and he served as president of the Jewish Welfare Federation of Greater Dallas.

He was also one of the pioneers of the American Israel Political Action Committee, which supported the people of Israel. AIPAC has grown into one of the most powerful lobbying organizations in the United States.

As in all things, Elsie and Stanley Pearle were full partners in their philanthropic work. Elsie was known as a classy, gracious hostess at the many fundraisers she organized at the Pearles' beautiful Dallas home. Surely her sincere warmth and spirited enthusiasm encouraged many a charitable donor to open their checkbook just a little wider.

Elsie participated in the same charities as her husband, but she also took part in several pet projects of her own. She was a member of various committees that supported the arts in Dallas and was active in various women's groups. She was active in the women's division of the Jewish Welfare Federation, and was also a national board member of the American-Israel Cultural Association.

"Elsie was a real humane person," said Dr. Pearle's former business partner, Bill Benedict. "They both did a lot to help people who needed it. They were really generous with their time and their assets."

Thanks to their involvement in Jewish causes and their support of Israel, during President Jimmy Carter's administration the Pearles were invited to a dinner at the White House given in honor of Israeli Prime Minister Menachem Begin.

"That banquet was quite an experience and one of the highlights of our public life," Dr. Pearle remembered. "It was a big deal. A dinner at the White House is quite elaborate, you know. We were in a beautiful room with people from different parts of the world. My wife sat at a table with the president, the prime minister and their wives, and I sat at a table with the secretary of state. It was just an unbelievable night."

Years later, in 1992, Dr. Pearle was awarded the State of Israel Medal of Peace, which acknowledged his significant impact on strengthening U.S.-Israel relations through fundraising, activism, service and leadership.

Today, Dr. Pearle is gratified that there's less anti-Semitism and discrimination in the United States than in the past, although he understands that there are pros and cons to the slow assimilation of Jews into mainstream society.

"In some ways there's less feeling about tradition and religion than there used to be," he says. "So some things are lost. It's good and it's bad in certain ways. Although segregation is not good, it *is* good for people with the same cultural values and interests to maintain their close ties."

Even though things have changed, Dr. Pearle believes it's just as important as ever for people to remain involved and not forget the past. He believes there's still hard work ahead, to ensure that trends toward increased acceptance and decreased discrimination continue, and to ensure that the unique culture and traditions of all people are protected.

Stanley Pearle's understanding of the discrimination often faced by Jews has always given him empathy for other cultural and racial minorities as well. During his years in Corpus Christi, a community with a large Latino and Hispanic population, he became increasingly aware of their causes. He was an active supporter of the American GI Forum, an organization dedicated to addressing problems of discrimination and inequities endured by Hispanic military veterans.

"It was new back then, but today it's extremely important politically," he explained. "My practice had a lot of Hispanics. But I was always sensitive to and interested in organizations that represented minorities, mainly because of my Jewish background. I was always interested in the Hispanic leaders down there, and I gave money to the GI Forum and tried to help them."

He also gave money to the civil rights movement in the African American community, and he continues to support various minority causes to this day.

Dr. Pearle's generosity did not stop there. He also gave time, money and effort to causes that benefited all sorts of people who needed a hand up: the sick, the disabled, the poor, the young, the elderly.

Bill Yost recalled, "Elsie used to laugh about how Stanley would have given away everything he owned if it weren't for her, and there was probably some truth in that."

While both Stanley and Elsie were extremely generous, many friends and family members have said that Elsie was often the voice of reason that held Stanley in check. She kept her eyes open for unscrupulous people who were just trying to milk her husband for money to pay for nonexistent, illegitimate or pie-in-the-sky causes.

According to his youngest daughter Roberta, "He was such

a soft sell. People were always asking him for help with fund raising. My mother used to say, after he sold the business, that he still needed to feel important."

No doubt, he *was* important to the many people whose lives were affected by his generous spirit.

Dr. Pearle became a board member for the Dallas chapter of the United Way and was named the first Jewish president of that organization in 1982. "Any organization that helps the underprivileged and the weak, I'm all for it, and I try to help them," he said.

He has also served as a member of the Dallas Citizens Council, a non-profit organization dedicated to the betterment of life in the city.

Whatever someone's religion, culture or politics, Dr. Pearle has always believed that it was important for all people to become involved in their communities. "I think it's important to elect the right leaders and sponsor the kind of causes you believe in. I believe very strongly that as a good citizen, you should be an active member of your community and country. Make sure you elect the kind of leaders that believe in the things you believe in."

According to Bill Yost, it was in the political arena that Dr. Pearle's generosity once almost got him into trouble, with his own party. "Dr. Pearle was a Democrat. There was a Republican convention in Dallas in the 1980s, and someone from that party asked him if he'd have a reception at his house. He said, 'Sure.' Some of his Democrat friends remonstrated and asked, 'Why are you throwing a party for the Republicans?'

"He said, 'I think Dallas should be hospitable to the people who are coming here. And I think that people should be supportive of the political process, and the political process in this country has two parties, not just one.'"

Yost always admired Dr. Pearle for that move. "Some people

would say he was a patsy. But I think it was not only a very generous thing to do, it was a smart thing to do. It was generous because the party was scratching around looking for a place, but it was smart because it was an opportunity for Stanley. You've got to realize his political instincts were sharply honed, because he'd been in the business of influencing legislatures for years. One thing he did was to stay friends with both parties. He didn't make enemies. And Stanley, by being a generous, good citizen of Dallas, was also affirming the fact that he was a very wise businessman. That's a sign of an intelligent man, someone who can do *well* by doing *good*."

Dr. Pearle also imbued Pearle Vision with his sense of civic duty, first as its founder and president, and later as its advisor and consultant. Under his guidance, the company has long been involved in philanthropic endeavors—most notably, the Pearle Vision Foundation, established in 1986.

The foundation awards grants to non-profit organizations nationwide, providing money for vision research and education. The goal of the research is to find better treatments and cures for diseases of the eye such as diabetic retinopathy and age-related macular degeneration—two leading causes of blindness and vision loss among Americans. The goal of the vision education is to provide ongoing training for optometrists.

Since 1986, the Pearle Vision Foundation has awarded more than $5.5 million to charities and individuals across the U.S. The grants that they awarded in 2005 included $10,000 for St. Jude's Children's Research Hospital in Memphis, Tennessee, to test new chemotherapy drugs for the treatment of retinoblastoma, a malignant tumor of the retina, and $25,000 for the Foundation of the University of Medicine and Dentistry of New Jersey, to study telecommunication technologies that could allow eye care specialists to diagnose and treat patients in remote locations.

To raise money for the foundation, Pearle used to sell lens cloths at its stores around the country. The foundation now receives an annual donation from Luxottica, the current owner of Pearle Vision; it also raises money through fundraisers, such as golf tournaments and silent auctions at franchise conventions.

For Dr. Pearle's 80th birthday, Pearle Vision held a special fundraising drive for the foundation. The company collected birthday card signatures in its stores in return for an 80-cent donation, and encouraged members of the optical industry to make $80 donations. At the birthday celebration, the company presented the good doctor with a $43,500 check made out to the foundation.

One of Dr. Pearle's favorite charitable activities—which was not run by the Pearle Vision Foundation—was a joint promotion involving Pearle Vision, the Boys and Girls Clubs and several big league baseball clubs. Each time one of the players hit a home run, Pearle Vision would give away a free eye exam and glasses to a needy child.

During that promotion, Dr. Pearle, a lifelong baseball fan and an excellent player in his own right, was able to make a personal fantasy come true—playing on a field with a major league team, if only for a moment.

"They invited me to Pittsburgh for one of the last games of the season," he explained, "to throw out the first pitch for the Pirates. We invited children from the Boys and Girls Club to the game, and it was on television. It was quite an event, another highlight of my life."

One reason that Luxottica has earned Dr. Pearle's respect is because of its dedication to public service. Not only does the company plan to continue donating funds to the Pearle Vision Foundation, but it also has another charitable arm, called Give the Gift of Sight. GGOS collects used glasses, recycles them and distributes them through free clinics around the world.

In total, GGOS has helped more than four million people since its inception in 1988. There's no better way to impress Dr. Pearle. "I like to be associated with companies that believe you need to give something back."

When he explains the importance of giving, it's clear that Stanley's wish to be of service is genuine, and does not come from a self-conscious desire to create a positive public image for himself. However, it's also clear that he believes that modern companies who do not give back to the community would do well to consider the effect on their images.

In business or out of it, Dr. Pearle has always believed that it's not possible to be successful without the twin values of honesty and charity.

"I'd like to believe that I've been a decent person and I've set a good example for people by living a decent life and giving something back to the community," he said. "I've heard people say they consider me a mentor, and I don't push that idea, but they may say it because they see me as a decent person with integrity, who is also dedicated to helping the weak and people who need help."

Former Pearle associate VP Dr. Smith found it refreshing that a man who rose from the working class neighborhoods of Depression-era Pittsburgh to become "a millionaire in the land of big hair and big diamonds" never felt the urge to put distance between himself and the humble world from which he came. Instead, Stanley Pearle took every opportunity to share his good fortune with those who didn't have as much.

Dr. Smith believed that because Dr. Pearle lived through the Great Depression and saw the kind of desperation that people could suffer, he understood the importance of compassion and the importance of people looking out for each other.

To Dr. Pearle, his dedication to mentorship and charity has always been no more, and no less, than the expression of his worthiest ambition. "I wanted to do good things in life. I wanted to do decent things. Some people call that being a do-gooder. I guess I was a do-gooder."

Faster Is Not Always Better

WHILE STANLEY WAS GETTING MORE INTERESTED in philanthropic affairs, Pearle was still growing, moving and shaking. It was acquired again in 1985, by Grand Metropolitan, PLC, an English food and beverage conglomerate. CEO Don Phillips exited the scene, and Grand Met sent in one of their own executives—Howard Stanworth—to take over the running of the company.

It was the first time a parent company got directly involved in operations. But still, even Grand Met found it important to keep Dr. Pearle involved as a marketing and public relations consultant. They had a good relationship.

But Dr. Pearle did not like *everything* the new owners came up with.

Pearle Vision faced no major competition until 1983, when LensCrafters came on the scene with a new marketing approach: one-hour service. The idea caught on with a time-conscious public, and LensCrafters pulled out front.

Stanworth tried to take on Pearle's new competition directly by matching their offer of one-hour service. He set up full labs in many of Pearle's already-profitable locations to accommodate the new service, which made those stores unprofitable.

Longtime Pearle franchisee Dr. Howard Oifer, who today owns 10 Pearle Vision offices in Atlanta, remembers jumping onboard the one-hour bandwagon. "I'm a competitive guy, and I wasn't going to let the competition do it without me. Back in the '80s, one-hour service came out in the top three most important customer services. I don't think it's even in the top 10 anymore, although we still offer it if people want it. That kind of service is only important for the guy who can't see two feet in front of him and has glasses that got chewed by the dog. But today, most people don't have time to wait around for an hour."

Said Dr. Pearle of Stanworth, "He was a wonderful guy, but looking back, it was a mistake trying to be something we weren't. We had a different type of format."

Today, the concept of one-hour service does not have the same impact on the industry as it did when it first came on the scene in the '80s. Since then, optical customers have renewed their interest in value, quality and service—the longstanding watchwords of Pearle Vision.

But even in those days, Pearle remained strong. In 1988, the company had around 1200 outlets, and brought in about $400 million in annual gross sales.

Stanley still believed that his company had the opportunity to carve a new niche by adhering more strongly than ever to its original principles. In other words, in some ways, everything old was new again.

Keeping On

IN 1996, PEARLE WAS ACQUIRED ONCE AGAIN—this time by Cole National Corporation of Cleveland, Ohio. Then, in 2004, it was adopted by its fifth and newest parent, Luxottica, Inc., one of the largest eyeglass frame manufacturers in the world. Luxottica also owned several other companies in the optical and fashion industries.

Although Dr. Pearle was by then semi-retired, he remained a valued company asset. His honesty and approachability made him a perfect ambassador for the Pearle brand. As his son David has said, Stanley never faked anything and because of that, people instinctively trusted him.

Dr. Jeff Smith noted that it was unusual in business to keep a founder on through so many changes in parent organizations. "When people met him and understood what he'd done, everyone came to the conclusion that he was someone they wanted to have in their camp. Even though he no longer held a formal position, when he walked into a room he still had more authority than anybody—he was someone people still responded to and wanted to listen to."

As Dr. Pearle saw it, "I guess each company has felt that I had a personality that was important from a morale standpoint and a motivation standpoint. Obviously, it's amazing that a company would keep a former executive for all these years. Here it is 2007 and I'm still involved. And we've already had five different parents. I never thought that I'd still be involved with the company after all these years."

Just as Pearle Vision continues to take pride in its founder, the founder continues to take pride in his company. "Even though I no longer have a large economic stake, I still have an emotional attachment to Pearle Vision because the company has my name. So I'm eager for it to be a good company, with a reputation for service and quality, because that's what I'm all about. I still feel bad when things are going badly, and very proud when things are going well."

As Bill Yost said, "Nobody in the history of business has stuck with a company after it was sold as long as Stanley has. I think it was loyalty and a feeling of pride in what he built."

These days, Dr. Pearle not only feels proud, but optimistic that Pearle Vision's new parent company is headed in a positive direction. "The other companies have been good, and all of them brought something to the table. But I'm more impressed with Luxottica than any of them. This company's marketing approach is not just about price, which has been a tendency of other companies in recent years, until it's almost become a price war out there. Luxottica instead wants to get away from making price the only consideration, and to convince people to come to Pearle for other reasons. They're emphasizing the company's professionalism and the quality of the products and the people. They're very people oriented. And they're playing up the idea that Pearle was founded by an optometrist."

Luxottica also owns other optical brands including LensCrafters and Sunglass Hut. Initially, some in the industry thought the new parent company might turn all the Pearle Visions into LensCrafters, but the company is excited about the Pearle name and the time-honored, trustworthy image it represents.

Not only is Dr. Pearle proud that his name will remain, he also thinks it's a smart idea. "They want to develop the brand more fully," he notes. "They understand that it's a well-known brand, thanks partly to the millions of dollars we spent over the years to market the Pearle name."

He is especially impressed that the new company is investing heavily in a new marketing strategy for Pearle Vision and is going over its existing stores with a fine-toothed comb to make sure they're performing in accordance with traditional Pearle values.

"They're going to lose some money on sales at first," Stanley speculates. "But that shows they're thinking in the long-term, and I'm very impressed with that. I think they'll be successful, judging from the success they've had with their other brands. They bought Sunglass Hut and they had a rough first year. But that's because they were changing the culture. The investment paid off, and now it's a very successful brand. Luxottica has been successful in understanding what each brand wants to do, and which customers they're trying to serve. I think they are the best parent we've ever had."

Luxottica is facing plenty of housecleaning as it seeks to

reinvigorate Pearle Vision's image with a strong injection of its original principles. "Quality of product and service and doing the extras, you've got to make sure the stores are providing that," he says. "Some of the franchisees have become lax about those things. They've got to make over the whole company and if necessary, get rid of some of the stores that aren't up to Pearle Vision standards. And they have to institute this culture of service."

Pearle Vision already has tremendous name recognition, but Luxottica is currently working on a marketing strategy to remind people of the *reputation* behind that name. Luxottica's goal is to remind customers that the Pearle brand represents friendly, professional service and high quality products.

Dr. Pearle is glad to see that the new Pearle Vision is more dedicated than ever to his original ideals—a culture of providing extra service, special attention and professional care.

"But if that's what you're promising," he adds, "you have to deliver it, if you want the public to respond, you see. And I believe the new owners understand that."

It's clear that Stanley's reputation is important to him, and that his reputation is tied up with his name, which the company still bears. Both Dr. Pearle and the new parent company recognize the value of his reputation in their marketing strategy. They believe customers are more likely to have faith in a company that the founder still stands behind long after he has ceased to have much financial interest in that company.

Dr. Pearle also points out that Pearle Vision has an advantage over many competitors because it can boast that it was founded by a professional optometrist.

Contacts Pop Up

PEARLE VISION'S EXCELLENT REPUTATION OVER THE YEARS has helped the company to be a true innovator in the field of optometry. The company was at the forefront of many new practices, services and products over the years—including the very controversial contact lens.

Plastic contact lenses were invented in 1948, and they slowly gained popularity in the 1950s and 60s, as they became thinner and lighter. The first soft contact lenses were introduced in 1971, and with that innovation, the market quickly took off.

But for years, regulations in many states made it tough for optical companies to reap all the benefits of the contact lens market.

Pearle Vision was one of the early pioneers to offer these fantastic new products to its customers. But inconsistent regulations from state to state made it difficult for them to turn it into a profitable operation.

"The laws got so strict with that," Dr. Pearle remembered. "As I've said, in many states we could not directly hire an optometrist, and the doctor's office had to be separate from the dispensary. This made it tricky because, by law, the doctors were the ones who had to handle the fitting, dispensing and servicing of the contact lenses. It became a little awkward for Pearle, because we made our money primarily from the dispensaries. So the rules inhibited our growth in that area to some degree."

In the past, while the independent doctor next door could send a patient to the dispensary with a prescription for glasses, he could not do the same with a contact lens prescription. So, Pearle Vision could only legally sell contacts in states where optometrists owned company franchises or worked directly for the company—in other words, in places where the dispensaries and the optometry practices were joint units.

"In our national advertising, which we got into pretty heavily, we couldn't say, 'Come to Pearle and we'll fit you for contact lenses and examine your eyes,' because in some states we weren't allowed to do that. It wasn't as simple as in the case of eyeglasses. In that case, we could say that we sold glasses and that an examination was available 'nearby.'"

Although a customer could get the contacts from the same nearby doctor, Pearle Vision couldn't advertise that because the company itself wasn't the one making the sale.

In 2004, that problem was eliminated when Congress passed a law requiring optometrists to release contact lens prescriptions to patients. So, Pearle customers can now fill their contact lens prescriptions at any dispensary they wish, just as they can with eyeglasses.

Dr. Pearle believed that the new rule would benefit both optical retailers and patients because dispensing contacts would be more efficient and cost effective, and because retailers would find it more worthwhile to compete for customers with lower contact lens prices.

But even before the regulations were eased, Dr. Pearle was positive on the subject of contact lenses as another great option for vision correction. "They're getting better all the time and the manufacturers keep improving the quality," he said. "The materials keep getting better, making them more comfortable, allowing tears to flow through them more freely, allowing them to be worn for longer or shorter periods. There's even talk of putting corrective lenses directly into the eyeball itself... Well, that's ophthalmology. But when contact lenses first came out more than 50 years ago, they weren't nearly as comfortable as they are now. They were hard, but people wore them anyway. My children all wore them. But they're so much better today."

An Eye for Fashion

IN RECENT YEARS, DR. PEARLE HAS BEEN PLEASED to see the eyewear industry expand beyond vision care to include a fashion focus. In the 1980s, he said, "Today, glasses are a fashion item. It's not uncommon to see movie stars and TV stars wearing glasses, and that was never the case 30 or 40 years ago. They're a style item today. People match glasses with their wardrobes."

In the 1990s he noted, "Fashion has become so key in eyewear that I think we'll see the day when someone will say, 'I've got $100 extra to spend on shoes, jewelry or eyeglasses to go with an outfit,' and the choice will be the extra pair of eyeglasses."

Dr. Pearle was right—that day has come. "In fact," he says now, "it's not uncommon for people to spend several hundred dollars for that extra pair of eyeglasses, because they find it the most important accessory to impact their overall look."

He calls the modern trends in eyewear design revolutionary, noting that until the fashion world began to take an interest in eyeglasses in the '60s and '70s, optometrists carried only 10 or 15 ladies' styles and 4 or 5 men's styles for patients to choose from. Today there are typically 800 to 1200 frames on display at vision stores, from every fashion designer you can think of.

Ironically, just when comfortable contact lenses and simple corrective surgery have made it possible for many people to correct their vision problems without glasses, now even those people who don't have vision problems actually *want* glasses. Eyewear is so "in" that many people with 20-20 vision buy frames fitted with clear, non-prescription lenses, just to accessorize a wardrobe or create a new look.

Although Dr. Pearle has been an innovator in vision care, when it comes to vision fashion, he says, "I was late on that one. I never thought style was that important an item when I started out. I did like the idea of providing a good selection of frames to customers, but for a long time our priority was price. You came to us to save money, get a good pair of glasses and a good examination. I never realized that style would be such a major factor in the retail business until maybe 10 to 20 years ago."

Although Dr. Pearle liked to say that he was a little late joining the fashion trend, a closer look revealed that statement as his classic humility. He was reluctant to take credit for anything for which he wasn't *fully* responsible. Of course, with many trends, no one person is responsible, but in the instance of the fashionable trend in eyewear, Dr. Pearle *did* play a part.

He actually did start paying attention to fashion in the 1950s, back when he joined forces with the now-defunct Lee Optical to open his first freestanding practice and dispensary.

"That first Dr. Pearle store was a good-looking place," he admitted. "We began preaching frame styles then. As a matter of fact, at our first store, we had one of the most popular frames, made by a company called Tura that still makes popular frames today. In those days, they made the most stylish type of frame there was. The designer was Monroe Levoy. He was way ahead of his time, one of the originators of style, a tremendous innovator. He was the first one who started fashion as a factor in the optical business. He had a program where he featured designing a frame around the contours of a person's face. And we put a Tura frame with diamonds on it in our window to attract customers."

Dr. Pearle said that it only made sense for someone to link eyewear with fashion, since back in the 1930s and '40s people purchased their glasses at jewelry stores. You might say that the answer was staring optometrists right in the face all along.

"Glasses cover one-third of your face," Stanley further reasoned, "so it makes sense that people consider them a fashion accessory, like jewelry. And today, many people look more attractive *with* glasses than without them. That never used to be the case in the old days. It's gratifying to see. Contact lenses and laser surgery have also done a lot to improve the appearance aspect of vision correction. That's progress, you know. But glasses are more attractive than ever."

Today, many optical service providers not only offer fashionable frames, they make them their primary focus, advertising that they have the best selection of designer eyewear. Many of the most respected names in the fashion industry have jumped into the frame manufacturing business—companies with names like DKNY, Chanel, Brooks Brothers, Prada, Versace and of course, Luxottica.

Dr. Pearle believed the importance of the customer's role in this trend should not be underestimated. "Today, the successful optical company has to address the fact that people are style conscious. That's still basic marketing—understanding what people are looking for, what motivates them."

Dr. Pearle noted that the fashion trend in eyewear provided many new marketing opportunities. When people started treating glasses like fine jewelry, the prices started to approach those of fine jewelry as well.

"When I first started in 1940," he recalled, "a pair of glasses was $10 to $15, including the exam. Today, the average price for the exam and the glasses can easily be $200 to $400. A good part of that is inflation, but it's much more than that, too. The quality is better, and the demand is greater.

"There *are* less expensive frames, and since people consider them fashion items, they often take advantage of the lower priced frames by buying more than one pair. They keep one by the phone, one in their desk, one in the car. They may even buy a different pair for special occasions or to match special outfits. Even people of modest means do it."

Given this fashion trend, Dr. Pearle believes that it's good news for Pearle Vision that its new parent company is a manufacturer of designer frames. "Luxottica makes gorgeous frames," he says. "They're true pieces of jewelry, you know. It's a big thing."

Luxottica also makes and markets sunglasses, another item that's rising on the charts of public demand. "The market is unbelievable," says Dr. Pearle. "Some people spend up to a thousand dollars for designer sunglasses. I've heard it said that fashion experts consider them one of the 10 fashion items that you must have."

Many of the style changes in eyewear have been made possible by evolving manufacturing techniques and the availability of modern materials. Lightweight plastics have made it possible to switch from clunky frames to lighter, airier styles. And the switch from those old, thick, "soda-bottle" glass lenses to such materials as polycarbonate have given those delicate frame styles something equally lightweight to wrap around.

"It's unbelievable how strong and thin they can make lenses with modern materials like polycarbonate," marvels Dr. Pearle. "And they make graduated bifocals so you can't see that horrible line. It's just marvelous how the optical industry has improved in the past 60 years. Without a doubt, even greater advances will be discovered in the next 60."

*Please join us
for a family reunion dinner
in celebration of*

Twins Merle (left) and Stanley (Buddy, right), circa 1921—They remained inseparable through childhood.

Merle and Stanley's birthday

*Friday evening, November 27 at 7:30 p.m.
Clair de Lune Restaurant
5934 Royal Lane
Dallas, Texas*

Stanley (Buddy, left), Merle (right), circa 1924—Although Buddy now says that Merle was the one more likely to pull a prank, at age six, it was Buddy who accidentally discovered how to release the brake on Uncle Phil's Model T.

Merle, Dorothy
(mother), Lester and
Stanley (Buddy) in
Atlantic City,
circa 1935.

Stanley (Buddy) on the Schenley High School baseball team (top
row, 5th from left)—He lettered in high school varsity baseball,
where he became a steady third baseman. "That was the greatest
achievement of my life."

Stanley (Buddy) and a friend, Harold Durshlag, at the Northern Illinois College of Optometry in Chicago— His instincts told him that pursuing an independent profession would be better for his long-term future.

Dr. Stanley Pearle graduates from optometry school, 1939—"I was going to be an optometrist and I wanted to look mature. So I grew a mustache."

Elsie & Stanley Pearle on their wedding day, September 10, 1940— She never doubted her decision to follow the man she loved to Texas. After she arrived, they were married the next day.

Elsie & Stanley Pearle, 1944—"She opened my eyes and made me realize that there's so much more to life than simply making a living."

Elsie & Stanley with
their first child,
David, 1944—"It was
a very difficult
labor... Men didn't
attend births in
those days, so I was
just pacing up and
down, sweating."

Stanley with son
David and
daughter Linda,
1945—Linda was
born in 1944.
Then the other
shoe dropped:
Stanley was
drafted.

Stanley and David Pearle, 1945—"He had heard I was in Pearl Harbor, so when people asked him his name, he replied, 'My name is David Lee Pearle Harbor.'"

Elsie & Stanley Pearle, 1945—One day there was a knock at the door, and she almost fell over when she saw her beloved husband standing there. Son David recalls, "She said it was 'the happiest day of her life.'"

Elsie and Stanley Pearle, vacationing in Acapulco, Mexico, 1956—
Roberta recalls, "He really believed marriage needed to be on an
even ground."

Elsie and Stanley Pearle, 19th wedding anniversary, 1959—Son Gary says, "I suspect that being married to someone who was at ease being affectionate in that way probably helped give him a reserve of confidence."

Stanley Pearle at the Wailing Wall in Jerusalem, circa 1960—"My generation lived through the Holocaust. I maintain that no Jew who lived during that time or who knew the history of the Jews could fail to be conscious of the importance of involvement in Jewish causes."

Dr. Stanley Pearle and his partner, Elsie Pearle, at the office, circa 1960—"She was always my partner as well as my wife and we discussed every decision."

Stanley Pearle heads the family table at the Seder dinner during Passover—Gary says, "Passover was always beautiful and there was always room for a large number of people."

Stanley Pearle with his grandson, Linda's son, Eric Levy, 1978—As with all people, Dr. Pearle has a knack for maintaining a unique relationship with each of his grandkids and great-grandkids, making each of them feel important to him as individuals.

Dr. Pearle attends a White House dinner with President Jimmy
Carter and First Lady Rosalynn Carter, circa 1977—During
President Jimmy Carter's administration, the Pearles were invited
to a dinner at the White House in honor of Israeli Prime Minister
Menachem Begin.

Dr. Pearle attends the opening of a new Pearle Vision store in the Netherlands, circa 1980—By the early '80s, Pearle Vision had the largest network of optical outlets in the world, with locations in the U.S., Puerto Rico, Mexico, Canada, Germany and the Netherlands.

Stanley and Elsie Pearle in Venice, Italy, circa 1980—Stanley learned to enjoy art and culture almost as much as his wife did.

Dr. Pearle in the 1980s—By the early '80s, according to a survey, when people were asked what company came to mind when they thought of eyeglasses, 8 out of 10 said "Pearle."

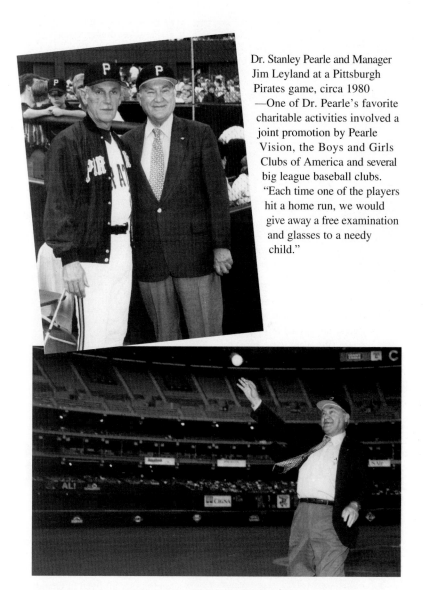

Dr. Stanley Pearle and Manager Jim Leyland at a Pittsburgh Pirates game, circa 1980 —One of Dr. Pearle's favorite charitable activities involved a joint promotion by Pearle Vision, the Boys and Girls Clubs of America and several big league baseball clubs. "Each time one of the players hit a home run, we would give away a free examination and glasses to a needy child."

Dr. Pearle throws out the first pitch at the same Pittsburgh Pirates game, circa 1980—"They invited me to Pittsburgh for one of the last games of the season, to throw out the first pitch for the Pirates. It was quite an event, another highlight of my life."

Elsie and Stanley Pearle getting ready for Passover dinner, circa 1980—Although the artwork she loved may have been museum quality, her home never felt like one. It was important to her that home was primarily a place for family.

The twins, Drs. Merle and Stanley Pearle, revisit the street where they grew up, circa 1980—Stanley says, "We were very close. He was a very warm, sensitive person and we had a wonderful relationship."

The home where Dr. Pearle grew up, as it looked circa 1980—Buddy, Merle, their two uncles, their mother and grandmother all lived in Grandma's skinny, three-story house in a working class neighborhood in Pittsburgh.

The Pearle brothers: Stanley, Lester and Merle, circa 1990—Sadly, the twins who had been so inseparable in their youth spent most of their adult lives many miles apart.

Elsie and Stanley Pearle, circa 1990—Elsie passed away in 1996. She was 77. "She was a wonderful partner my whole life and I still miss her."

Dr. Pearle pouring champagne on Elsie Tulips at the official naming of the new tulip variety at The Hague, the Netherlands, 1996—The Netherlands division of Pearle Vision had decided to have a new tulip named after her. "They're her favorite color, which is passionate pink," Stanley says.

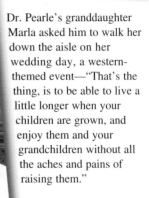

Dr. Pearle's granddaughter Marla asked him to walk her down the aisle on her wedding day, a western-themed event—"That's the thing, is to be able to live a little longer when your children are grown, and enjoy them and your grandchildren without all the aches and pains of raising them."

Chapter 6

The Life of a Leader

DR. PEARLE NEVER FORGOT THE DEBT HE OWED to the Boy Scouts of America for providing him with mentors who instilled important moral values in him and taught him how to set and achieve goals. Not only did he attain the advanced rank of Life Scout as a boy, you might say that, as a man, he continued to take the title to heart, remaining a scout throughout his life.

He's given back to the community by becoming a mentor to many of the people he's met in both professional and private life, and by giving much of his time, effort and money to many charitable causes.

On the occasion of Dr. Pearle's 80th birthday, Dave Pierson, president of then-parent company Cole National said, "He has offered personal and professional counseling to more people in eye care than probably any other individual—when I can't get hold of my own dad for advice, I call Dr. Pearle."

Mentoring

THOSE PEOPLE WHO DR. PEARLE HAS TAKEN under his wing say he's not only taken an interest in their medical and business educations, but their personal lives as well. This is perhaps an easy shift, because Dr. Pearle tries to apply the same principles to business as he does to private life.

According to Dr. Smith, Stanley's attitude is. "Take care of yourself. But by the same token, when you're in business, also take care of others."

It is well known that Dr. Pearle's advice is never tainted with ego. "When he shares his opinion," says Dr. Oifer, "he never delivers it with the attitude of 'I've been in this business for so long and you should listen.' I have had other mentors— and sometimes a mentor, to me, is more like a teacher, more formalized, directing me through the labyrinth of corporate America. But with Dr. Pearle, it has been very informal. It has been a friendship. He has stature, yet he's incredibly sociable. We've gone together to see his daughter at the opera or gone out to share a meal, things like that. He's just a wonderful person to hang with. I think I appreciate that as much as the business learning."

Although Dr. Pearle is not usually aggressive about giving advice, he can be very assertive when he's concerned about the well being of his friends. Dr. Smith says, "There have only been two times I can remember that he had the attitude of 'you should know this.' The first was when he gave me advice about drinking and driving. I was talking about going out somewhere and he looked at me and said, 'Have enough sense that if you're having a wonderful evening drinking, you take a cab home.'

"The second was when I was traveling a lot. He asked, 'Are

you taking care of yourself, Jeff? Have you had an annual exam? Are you watching your weight?' He used to travel a lot, too, and he knew how difficult it could be to stay in shape, what with flying and staying at hotels and eating out. He has the same problem I do—we both love food and we both can pack on the weight. I think that when he was traveling, he learned to make time for exercise. Those were the only two times he was very direct, and he was right.

"Other times, he just made suggestions, like a consultant. Often older friends and older family members can tend to be preachy, but that is not Dr. Pearle. He never tells me what to do."

Family is important to Dr. Pearle, and he's extended his mentorship there as well, and not just to his children. Even though Stanley and Elsie left Pittsburgh behind, their family ties there always remained strong. In spite of the distance, Elsie's nephew, Chuck Cohen, discovered a special connection with Stanley, his closest uncle, respected mentor and beloved friend.

"There's always a feeling of warmth when he's around," Chuck says. "I still refer to him as Uncle Buddy."

At times when Chuck had difficulties relating to his own father, Uncle Buddy stepped in to listen and advise, treating him like a son. Whenever he visited, he always made Chuck feel like someone special.

"We knew Uncle Buddy was a busy and important guy, but when he spoke with an individual, it was as if not a thing was going on in the world except him listening to the person who was talking to him. So if I was in junior high school and talking about what I was doing on my little league team, that was the most important thing to him at the moment."

As with many of Dr. Pearle's friendships, he and Chuck spent a lot of time bonding over sports. "He was a big Pirates fan, so I have memories of going to games with him when I was young. That was a big connection."

One of Chuck's fondest memories was when Uncle Buddy came to his Bar Mitzvah. "Keep in mind that this was 1958, when flying was a much bigger deal. The notion of him flying from Texas to Pennsylvania to come to my Bar Mitzvah was a tremendous deal to me."

Chuck worked his way through college without financial support from his parents, but Uncle Buddy and Aunt Elsie often gave him financial assistance to help him get through. When he graduated, they flew out for the event, which again meant a great deal to Chuck.

Chuck went on to law school and after he received his degree, Dr. Pearle invited him down to Dallas to interview for a job with his company. Chuck spent nine months working as a counsel for Pearle Vision before starting a legal career in Washington, DC.

Later, Chuck's father, who was to be his best man at his wedding, passed away shortly before the event. There was no question who he would ask to step in as best man—of course, it could be none other than Uncle Buddy.

When the Pearle kids grew up, for several years, the Pearles rented a villa in Acapulco every Christmas. The kids and their spouses, boyfriends and girlfriends were all invited, and so was Chuck. "I was favored with invitations to go down there. My wife and I would go, even before we were married."

When Stanley extends his friendship to someone, it goes beyond that person to include his or her family and loved ones. "He has a special bond with my children, and he's a friend to my friends," says Chuck. "They all call him Uncle Buddy."

Chuck says it's easy to understand why so many people are attracted to the simple warmth that his uncle spreads wherever he goes. "He is totally unaffected. Here's this very successful person who is caring about the problems of whoever he's talking to, and there's no bull involved, just what you see is what you get."

To this day, Chuck and his Uncle Buddy still keep in frequent touch.

Dr. Pearle has not only been a mentor to family members and people who've worked with him, but to many who've simply been lucky enough to happen across his path.

Dr. Phillip S. Wolf is not an optometrist, but a cardiologist and professor of medicine at the University of Colorado Health Sciences Center. He met Stanley and Elsie Pearle when he was a young boy in Corpus Christi, Texas, in the 1940s. The Pearles were close friends of his parents.

"Even at that time, Stanley played an important role in my life. He took me to baseball games," Dr. Wolf remembers. "His favorite phrase was, 'He needs to hustle.' That's what he'd say if a second baseman was too slow getting the ball to first or something like that. 'He's got a lot of hustle' is a favorite quote of his about people who impress him."

Dr. Wolf remembers one time when he was about 12 and their families were gathered together to celebrate the Jewish High Holidays. He and Stanley wanted to catch the final game of the World Series on the radio.

"The Cleveland Indians were playing the Boston Braves. This was in the pre-television days, in 1948, and the final game of that series was broadcast on the radio. We really wanted to hear the game uninterrupted, so we snuck out to the driveway to sit in his car, which was a green 1946 Plymouth, and we listened to the entire game on his car radio. The Indians won, four to three."

Dr. Pearle and young Phillip had shared an historic moment; that was the last time Cleveland won a World Series.

Stanley always made young Phillip feel like a member of his family. "'Avuncular' is a good word for him," the younger man says. "He's like an uncle, but he's also a multi-dimensional friend. A lot of kids look to a person who's older for guidance.

I always thought him to be a steadfast and dependable guide. But even though he was 18 years older, he was never patronizing. I would talk to him when I was a young person, in my teens, because I found him a very steadying influence. He was, and is, self-possessed without being arrogant. He practiced ethically in his work, and his advice was based on good faith and good morals."

Later, as a young man, Phillip reconnected with Dr. Pearle, when they were both living in Dallas in the 1950s. Stanley's career was taking off, and young Phillip was just starting medical school.

Stanley and Elsie were tremendously supportive throughout his years at school, and when he graduated, Elsie threw a huge dinner party for him, in her own generous and inimitable style.

But the support of the Pearles went deeper than that. When Dr. Wolf got married and began his residency, Elsie and Stanley understood that the young couple was in for a rough start. "My wife and I were poor as mice and we lived on the wrong side of the tracks, and the Pearles took us under their wing," Phillip remembers. "They really befriended us. They fed us well and really took care of us. We were always in their home. It probably wasn't easy to take a young hungry resident and his two kids into their home, but there was never a word that it was inconvenient. They always initiated it—we would never presume to call and ask. They were intuitive enough to know when we weren't doing that well."

Although the Pearles were quite wealthy, and the Wolfs lived on "the wrong side of the tracks," the former never let the latter feel the difference. Dr. Wolf explains, "They always treated us as equals even though we lived in Oak Cliff, home of Lee Harvey Oswald, and they lived in North Dallas, in a lovely home. Their generosity was not just financial. They really gave of themselves."

Although Dr. Pearle was thrilled to help out, he would not presume to give unsolicited advice. Yet Dr. Wolf respected his older friend's opinion, so when he and his wife considered buying their first home, he put his faith in Dr. Pearle's financial savvy and called him for advice.

"I wasn't making any money," Dr. Wolf says. "I was still in training, and I didn't know if it was something I should take on. So I talked to Stanley about going into debt. He said, 'Absolutely. If you can do it, you should do it.' He told me that my present was not my future. He explained that going into some degree of debt was okay. On the basis of that reassurance, we took the plunge. We bought a very modest home, but we took the plunge."

It was one of the few times Dr. Pearle gave his friend direct advice—that just isn't his way. Instead, he's usually the type who leads by example.

"I've found him to be a role model for my own behavior," says Dr. Wolf. "He's had financial setbacks in life, but he handles them well. He has a lot of confidence in himself without being swaggering. He's very involved in the community and helping others, but he keeps a very even keel. He does everything with a lot of equanimity and aplomb."

Over the years, Dr. Wolf has become successful in his own right, but the generous friendship of Stanley Pearle remains a constant. After 60 years, the two still talk frequently on the phone, and they visit whenever Dr. Wolf is in Dallas. "I value his friendship, and I would say loyalty for him is a prize attribute," Phillip says. "He has never wavered in his loyalty to my wife and me and our family. I feel we are family."

Once someone enters Dr. Pearle's circle of friendship and trust, it's a bond that lasts for life. Dr. Oifer also calls him regularly. "We've become close personal friends and have a mutual caring about each other that has transcended business," he says. "To this day, we still try to talk every couple of weeks. Even though he's not my family, I end every conversation by telling him that I love him and that we're thinking of him."

Dr. Oifer took Dr. Pearle to the Super Bowl in Atlanta in 1994, to watch the Dallas Cowboys defeat the Buffalo Bills. They spent the entire weekend together, along with Dr. Pearle's son David and grandson Andy.

Dr. Oifer bought them all the coveted tickets to the biggest Super Bowl parties, as well as the games. "I always appreciated him and wanted to show my appreciation," he says. "And I still believe that if I really needed something, I could call him up and he'd find a way to do it for me."

Dr. Pearle has already proven him right. "When my father-in-law got sick with lung cancer," Dr. Oifer says, "he needed to get into the M.D. Anderson Cancer Center in Houston. But there was a three-month waiting list. I called Dr. Pearle and told him the problem we were having. He said he'd take care of it. In 30 minutes, he called a former governor of Texas for me and called me back to say that the hospital's head of patient relations would meet us at the airport. He said we could take my father-in-law right over. Dr. Pearle would never tell you he would do anything unless he was sure he could do it."

Stanley has always made an effort to offer encouragement and support to family, friends and colleagues, but that is only the beginning of a deep well of compassion for everyone he meets.

Dr. Pearle is a man used to rubbing elbows with great leaders: state lawmakers, U.S. senators, governors and presidents. Yet he's not intimidated, nor is his head turned, by people in power. "I can't say that I don't enjoy some of it," he says. "It's nice. But it doesn't overly impress me. Some people live and die by that sort of thing—shaking hands and getting autographs. It was never a big deal in my life."

Stanley has been a power broker over the years himself as

well. He's well known throughout the optical field, and in the business world at large, as a great leader and a pioneer of the optical retail revolution. During the Pearle Vision national advertising campaigns of the '80s, in which he frequently appeared on camera, he became something of a celebrity, too. Today, he's still quite famous in the company he founded—a figure of almost mythic proportion.

Yet none of it has ever gone to his head. "I keep saying to myself that I'm just a very fortunate person," he says humbly. "I have good health and a good family, and I built a good business. And I'm very grateful for it."

Although Dr. Pearle attributes much of his success to luck, he does believe there's a right path and a wrong path to take to meet one's luck. "It's important to be ambitious," he says, "but you should also respect your friends and not tramp on other people. I'm not deeply religious, but I believe in the Ten Commandments—it's just as simple as that. That's my religion as far as I'm concerned. To be an honest, decent person is very important in life. That's what I've tried to teach."

Pearle's Wisdom

ALTHOUGH STANLEY PEARLE DOES NOT BELIEVE in preaching to others, he's happy to be asked for his advice and enjoys sharing his opinion. "He always scolds himself for rendering opinions," says his nephew Chuck. "But his instincts are dead on and what he says always makes a whole lot of sense."

When Dr. Pearle shares his philosophies of life and business with others, they often take the form of simple aphorisms. That's probably because he truly believes that the key to happiness and success is to live and work according to a few basic values.

To business people, he offers such phrases as: "One of the secrets of growing is to attract and keep good people," or "the secret to success in retail is good marketing."

To family members, he often repeats such gems as, "Appreciate every phase of your life," or "These are life's precious moments."

But as a leader and mentor, Dr. Pearle is much more than a walking book of axioms. To understand his philosophies truly, one need only look at the way he's lived his life. His strong sense of ethics, service and mentorship have earned him many friends and admirers who believe he is a true example to others

In all areas of Stanley's life—work, family and community—there is a simple clarity to his values and ideals that would easily lend themselves to a guidebook for living. Such a book would offer simple wisdom on subjects like the role of integrity on the road to success, how to set and achieve goals, and the nature of leadership.

Ask people who know Dr. Pearle to describe him and the two ideas that come up most often are extraordinary honesty and warm friendliness.

"He listens more than he talks," says Bill Yost. "And he's absolutely a straight-shooter, absolutely honest, and a very generous man, a kind person. Stanley is a man who doesn't have a lot of pride about him. He is what he is. I think that comes through in all his business dealings, as well as in his personal life."

Stanley's psychologist son, Dr. Gary Pearle, remembers one key moment that he believes unlocks a door to understanding his father's knack with people: "At the Bar Mitzvah of my younger son Brian, my dad had to get up in front of everyone and recite a Hebrew prayer, and he completely mangled it. Rather than getting uptight or nervous, he simply looked at the crowd and said, 'Doesn't it just go to show you what a great thing Brian has done? It shows you how hard this is.'

"After hearing that, the rabbi, who'd known Dad for years, felt free to joke, 'All I can say is, it's a good thing I'm in the forgiveness business.' So the formal ritual was informed by my dad's unselfconscious way with it. He used his own fallibility to enrich my son's Bar Mitzvah experience."

As a psychologist, Gary offers a unique insight into Dr. Pearle's humility and his unaffected, unembarrassed willingness to poke fun at himself in a way that allows other people to shine. "It is effective in group psychology to understand your own limitations and have a certain transparency. He comes by all that naturally. It's a true value. He doesn't have anything to hide. He isn't out there at your expense. He doesn't want to flourish at your expense. He wants to do a good job for you. So there's no need to dissemble, because he isn't hiding anything."

Gary says that his father's ability to be completely at ease with himself has had a profound influence on his own life. "It's not as if I grew up having him very near me. Yet the ripple effects of that attitude are very profound."

Dr. Pearle's youngest child, Roberta, says that her father used to put the idea very simply. "He used to say, 'I'm like Popeye. I yam what I yam.'"

Roberta believes that one of the great things about her father's wisdom is that it does not come from some high and lofty place. "There's something a little childlike about him," she says. "It's refreshing the way he boils things down to simple terms—like, 'Do the right thing.' Because he puts things simply, you always know where you stand.

"Another thing he likes to say—whenever any of us have had problems with other people, he's always encouraged us with, 'Just talk things out, reason with them.' He's really big on working things out one-on-one with people."

Although he is excellent at making people feel empowered in face-to-face communication or in small groups, Dr. Pearle's desire to be of service and to help others become successful reaches all the way to the world stage. "He wants world peace," says Roberta. "It's coming from an altruistic place."

If there is any flaw in her father's outlook, Roberta believes it is only that when other people present him with exciting new business ideas or new philanthropic ventures, he sometimes forgets that not everyone is as transparent, honest and altruistic as he is. "He's trusting," she says. "Sometimes too trusting— sometimes I think we have to protect him a little bit."

Dr. Pearle admits that it's true, and he says that's one reason he used to rely heavily on Elsie's input whenever making a decision to become involved in a new venture. Even in this, though, he provides a role model, showing the importance of knowing one's own limitations, and relying on trusted advisors to fill in those gaps.

In any case, the rewards that he, his business and his charitable ventures have reaped from his faith in others have far outweighed the costs.

Certainly the faith he and his wife had in each other created an enviable marriage that was as nearly perfect as they come. Stanley stresses the importance of treating marriage as an equal partnership. He and Elsie deeply loved each other and just as important, they deeply respected each other. Every decision they made, they made in concert.

Stanley has also talked to his children and grandchildren about the importance of faithfulness in a marriage. He's not shy about telling people that he was always faithful to Elsie. "I never wanted to do anything that would have made me feel terrible if she did it," he says. "On the other hand, I think it has to do with the fact that we were happy and content. Being faithful was never a problem for me. It was easy. We were in love, and deeply. I respected her so much. She was a good person."

While Stanley and Elsie had very different personalities, they also had much in common. "She was interested in the same things I was interested in, as far as community involvement." Stanley believes that their having common values was more important than their having different *interests*.

If she was more of a live wire who was into the arts, and if Stanley was more of an easygoing guy who was interested in work and sports, he saw these differences as opportunities for each of them to grow. Elsie introduced him to a side of life he would not otherwise have experienced, and vice versa.

Although Dr. Pearle maintains a calm exterior and is very easygoing in his dealings with people, Dr. Wolf observes that there's more to his friend and mentor than that. "There's an old saying that a successful person is like a duck—smooth and calm on the surface, but paddling like hell underneath. That's Dr. Pearle."

And Stanley doesn't mind giving other people advice on how to improve their own "paddling." Over the years, he has always been willing to tell people when they needed to change something to improve their performance. But it always comes from his desire to help—an employee, a friend, a customer or anyone who needs it.

Completely unselfconscious, he'll even offer helpful advice to a stranger. Nephew Chuck recalls, "We used to go to a lot of baseball games together, and I remember there was a time when he thought a particular Pirates player was doing something at the plate that was not helpful. He actually sent a letter to that player suggesting that he do something that would correct what he was doing wrong with his swing. I guess I'd say that there's no guile with Stanley at all—what you see is what you get. He had a thought, so he offered it."

Son David also recalls an example of his father's ability to relate comfortably to people, without self-consciousness or pretense. It happened when his father came to visit him at Amherst. "We were walking down the street, and Robert Frost was walking a few steps ahead of us. I said quietly, 'Dad, that's Robert Frost, the greatest American poet.' Then, because Dad and I were both big baseball fans, I added, 'And, you know, he used to be quite a baseball player.' Well, that really grabbed his interest.

"So right then my dad walked right up to him and said, 'Mr. Frost, I understand you're quite a ball player.' I was ready to sink into the sidewalk, but he ended up being charmed by my father. We actually went into the hotel and sat down together and talked. Dad just has that way with people."

Roberta, the youngest, also admires her father's easy way with people. "All the Pearle Vision franchisees talk about him being someone they look up to, but he also has a sweet and gentle way about him. He's very charismatic—when he walks into a room people want to talk to him. And he enjoys it as much as they do. He always wants to be part of something bigger than himself, and he likes being part of this optical revolution."

To his younger son Gary, Stanley has always been an inspiration, a role model of the quintessential self-made man. "One of my memories of him, during the time when he was building the business, was of being in his office," Gary says. "There was a map of the U.S. with all these push pins in it, representing the stores he had opened around the country. I remember having a sense of how he had gotten that far, step-by-step, from going to school during the Great Depression, to learning how to be a doctor, to opening his first office.

"He started with nothing, and not just financially nothing. His father left the family before he was born, and his mother was not an educated woman. He started without money, and without a family who knew what little boys needed in terms of emotional support. Yet step by step, he just moved forward, married a beautiful and extraordinarily intelligent woman and grew a successful business. It's impossible for that *not* to be an inspiration. It's so quintessentially American—the idea that who you're going to become is not predetermined, but has to do with your own abilities and your willingness to invest yourself in something."

But, like David, what most impressed Gary were not his father's achievements in themselves, but the consistency of character he exhibited along the way. "What he modeled for me was a basic sense of ethics: honesty, loyalty and responsibility."

Both Stanley and Elsie armed their children with a sense of core values, but at the same time gave them the freedom to be themselves and find their own ways.

Elsie and Stanley always commanded respect from their children without having to ask for it directly. They asked their children only for such simple things as having good manners, being considerate of other people's feelings, turning off the lights when they left a room and not swearing.

Roberta, the youngest, laughs as she recalls, "When they wanted to keep me from hearing things, they would speak in Yiddish. It was a very civilized home, and I was very grateful for that. Dad liked a peaceful home."

Her father sought that peace for himself, too, as much as for anyone else. Roberta says, "He would come home and take a nap every single day—he called it a catnap. I think it really contributed to his health."

The children all remember that their father's style of discipline took the form of influence, rather than demands. Roberta says, "He would get upset if we wore make-up, but he didn't tell us not to. He would just say, 'Why are you putting on that war paint?'"

Later, when Linda decided to get married and start raising a family before she finished college, her parents were clearly not happy, but they did not stand in her way. "I wouldn't say he didn't try to influence us," Linda says. "You knew if he disapproved of something you did. But he always stood by you, whatever you decided."

According to Stanley, "We just had confidence in the kids and we let them make their own decisions and encouraged them. They were good children, and they weren't hard to handle, so we didn't have to enforce anything. I wasn't a great preacher to the kids, and neither was Elsie. I never liked it when people preached to me, either."

Later, when Roberta left college after her third year to study opera in Europe, her parents both gave her their blessing. She had a beautiful voice, and they were very proud of her. But joy in their daughter's accomplishment nearly turned to tragedy, just six months after she arrived in Vienna, Austria.

Roberta was in a horrific car accident. She was the passenger in a car that was hit by a drunk driver. She was seriously injured, with a severe concussion, a large gash in her head and four broken bones, including her femur, the largest bone in the body. It took two surgeries to repair it.

Stanley remembers receiving the terrifying phone call. "As a parent, it's a terrible thing to get a call like that early in the morning. I grabbed the first plane I could to get to Vienna."

Berta was touched by the speed of her father's response. "I swear he was there within 12 hours—like, how could that even be possible?!"

But she was soon as amused as ever by her father's way of trying to make the best of a bad situation. He stayed for many days, during which Roberta had numerous visitors, and, of course, her dad engaged all of them in lively discussions.

"The guy who had been driving the car was Egyptian and one of my friends was Lebanese, and this was in 1976, when Jimmy Carter was heavily involved in the Middle East peace process and the Palestinian crisis. So here I am in this dreary hospital room, surrounded by people, and my dad would join them in these constant political discussions about world peace over the top of my arm, which was up in traction. And he would eat all my meals. I hated the hospital food, and Dad always had a robust appetite. I must have lost 30 pounds."

Nonetheless, she was grateful for her dad's caring attention. In time, Roberta healed. Another parent might have reacted by becoming overprotective and trying to convince his child to come home, but her father never tried to sway her independent course.

However, forever after, as each of his grandchildren have approached their 16th birthdays, they have all received a short lecture from Stanley on safe driving. "That's a big bugaboo with me," he says, "to teach kids that when you get behind the wheel, your life could be snuffed out, just like that. It's a wonderful time of your life, enjoy it and appreciate it, but remember when you get behind that wheel that's the time to be careful, that's not the time to kibitz around."

It's the closest thing to a stern lecture that the easy-going Stanley ever gives to young people.

As for Roberta, she stayed in Vienna for four years and went on to establish and manage a summer opera company in Boston.

The Perfect Marriage

STANLEY AND ELSIE PEARLE WERE NOT JUST ROLE MODELS of character, civility and strength; they were also role models of a strong marriage. "They loved to dance," Roberta says. "They went out every single Saturday night that I could recall. They loved to go to theatres, parties, weddings, Bar Mitzvahs, the club. They had a lot of respect for each other; there was never any disrespectful talk between them."

Stanley Pearle was an attractive, charismatic man, and

when he was on the road, he certainly received attention from women. But he volunteers the information that he never even considered giving in to temptation. "I was in love with my wife and very deeply. I knew there were married people who traveled a lot who fooled around. But I always asked myself how I would like it if my wife did the same thing to me. I never did it in my life."

"It was a lifelong love affair, no question," David says. "You just had to see them together to realize it. My parents were very different people, but they respected each other. I'm sure it was a very physical relationship. But they were also partners in business. When they started the company she was his most valuable executive."

Linda believes her mother played an integral role in the success of Pearle Vision. "My mother not only held it together for the family at home, but also at the office."

Dr. Pearle's longtime associate and friend, Bill Yost, says of Elsie, "She was a remarkable lady. She was a great counterbalance for Stanley, because she was tough-minded. Talk about being insightful, holy heck! This lady knew that business."

Stanley would not dispute that. "Elsie had a good feel for marketing and in the early days she used to come in quite a bit. Even after that, she was always my partner as well as my wife and we discussed every decision. She was this tremendous guidance in my life—there was no question about that—as well as being a great mother."

While money made life easier for Stanley and Elsie, it did not turn their heads. They lived well, but not ostentatiously. Stanley had never felt a driving desire for the finer things; he simply wanted to provide for his family, and to play a part in something vital and important. As for Elsie, Stanley says, "She wasn't overly interested in clothes, and she never wore diamonds, didn't like them at all."

However, the success of Pearle Vision meant that Elsie could finally indulge her long interest in art. Stanley frequently took her on trips to New York, to go to concerts and plays and visit art museums. "She could spend all day at the Guggenheim and the Museum of Modern Art. That was her greatest thrill," he recalls, smiling.

Meanwhile, at home, she amassed quite a collection of elegant and valuable modern art. With the eye of a professional curator, she would buy a piece at $20,000 that would increase to $400,000 dollars in value.

The Pearles also decided to build their dream home, and Elsie spent a year working closely with the architect on the design. The family moved into the new house in 1972. It was more than 4000 square feet, an elegant but modern structure with clean lines and plenty of light, and it appeared in several magazines. "It was Elsie's creation, and it was just a gorgeous home," Stanley says with pride, always eager to give credit where it is due. "People used to say it was one of the classiest modern homes in Dallas."

Longtime friend Phillip Wolf recalls, "Every room had one wall that was glass, and that wall looked out on greenery. The other walls featured magnificent, museum-quality art. The home was a showpiece—never garish, but with great taste. Elsie had an eye for art. It was also a house full of books that were being used, which told me a lot."

It was easy to see that this was a home owned by people who cared about art and knowledge, people who were interested in gaining a better understanding of the world in which they lived.

While Elsie loved beautiful things, her home was always warm and inviting, and although the artwork she loved may have been museum-quality, her home never felt like a museum. It was important to her that home was primarily a place for family.

Her daughter Linda recalls her special warmth toward children. "If something was broken by a child—and sometimes they were nice things that other people would have been devastated to lose—my mother always said, 'It's just a thing, it doesn't matter.' To her, it was the child that mattered."

Stanley learned to enjoy art and culture almost as much as his wife did. He believes those interests made him a more well rounded person, a concept he tried to pass on to his children. Stanley says, "I used to tell my children that it's important when they go to college the first year or two to just open up the windows with a little liberal arts and stuff like that, before they focus on making a living, which I did from the time I was a teenager. There's so much more to life than just making a living—to learn about the arts and philosophy, to be able to walk down the street and see beauty around you. And our children do have artistic ability, which I think they got primarily from Elsie."

The Pearles were also believers in community involvement, and generosity to those less fortunate than themselves. Elsie combined those qualities with her wonderful taste and appreciation for beauty. She loved to entertain, opening her beautiful home for fundraising activities and networking to help others.

Gary remembers how his mother expressed both her generosity and her love of beauty by befriending one young teenager. "She was a very underprivileged Hispanic girl, an artist who my mother mentored and invited to the house a number of times. My mother supported her efforts, gave her emotional support, bought a lot of her sculptures and connected her with people who could help her. My mother was not an artist herself, but she fell into the role of nurturing other people's talents. She was excited to discover who you were, what you did, what you were interested in. To her, it was like you were giving her a gift."

Elsie gave the same support to her own children's artistic

endeavors. Her two youngest, Roberta and Gary, became very involved in theatre during high school, and they joined a summer stock group in Dallas. "She was always willing to invite the entire crowd over for a cast party," Gary says. "And she always laid out this extraordinary array of food—you know how much teenagers eat. She would always make welcome this motley and sometimes difficult crowd. That was in the 60's. It was a time of tremendous anxiety around teenagers, but there was this larger embrace that she had. She admired what they did and made it clear that 'of course they should come over.' There was this sense that whatever was going on, she could nurture and share in it. Not that she felt a need to hang out with the kids—there was a balance.

"Both my mom and Dad made room for all of this in a way that gave all of us an invitation to express ourselves in a very different way," Gary goes on. He remembers that both his parents gave him a stable, supportive, loving environment in which to grow. "I honestly had this sense that if I was appropriately considerate of other people, then if there was something really important that I wanted to say or do or get, it would be respected."

An Elegy for Elsie

DR. PEARLE HAS LIVED A LIFE FREE OF REGRETS. Unfortunately, no one can live a life free of loss. However, he has been lucky enough to attract the kind of amazing people in his life who make it difficult to say goodbye.

His wife was such an integral part of his life that he found saying goodbye almost impossible. Stanley and Elsie Pearle were married for 57 years and to Stanley, it was his longest and strongest partnership. "We had no secrets from each other. We were great. There was nothing that I would hesitate talking to her about and vice-versa."

They had very different personalities, but very similar values, and it seems that it was that combination of similarities and differences that made them so compatible. "She was well-read, very intelligent. I admired the fact that she had a taste in the beauties of life. She was interested in the arts, in music. She didn't play an instrument but she loved to go to the opera and go to the symphonies and things. I was limited in that respect, so one-sided. I liked the fact that she liked those things, which I needed to be exposed to a little more. On the other hand, she was also interested in social problems, as I was, in fighting discrimination and helping others. So in other ways she had the same interests I had, you see."

Dr. Phillip Wolf recalls, "I think they had a truly loving relationship. They were different personalities, obviously. Elsie was the human dynamo, and Stanley was and is a more placid person, but I thought there was great mutual respect and I think their oars were in the water in the same direction. They shared the same values. Elsie was more sociable, I think, and Stanley was much more involved in developing the business, but their core values were identical."

Their son Gary says, "It was one of those marriages that was based on complimentary natures, because they *were* very different. My dad will say in his more concrete way that she introduced him to this artistic world. But I think she introduced him to this more creative, emotional side of himself."

She introduced her husband and children to their spiritual sides as well. Elsie did not grow up in a very religious household, but when she married, she was determined to maintain strong Jewish traditions and a life of faith in her own home. Stanley fondly remembers the warmth those traditions added to their lives.

"The Friday night Sabbath was important. It was where we lit candles and said prayers, and all the Jewish holidays were always big events—Passover and Yom Kippur. We celebrated all of the Jewish holidays. So the children grew up very conscious of Judaism."

Dr. Howard Oifer admired the relationship between Stanley and Elsie. "Obviously he truly loved her. He took his marriage to her very seriously and he treated her as a partner whose opinion he valued. She'd always counsel him and he'd always listen. They had a very unique relationship, the kind of relationship that people always talk about wanting. I think she truly was his best friend."

It's perhaps ironic that Elsie was the first to go, since she took the greatest interest in both her health and her husband's. "She enjoyed cooking, until I got heavy and began worrying about my weight. She frequently put me on a diet. She was never heavy. She was very up on reading all the books on health, she was careful about what she ate and she did a lot of exercise to stay in shape. She was almost a health nut."

Yet her interest in health excluded seeking the advice or care of a doctor—another irony for a woman whose husband was a health professional, and whose eldest son was a physician.

"She never would get a physical exam," Stanley says. "She had a hang-up—she refused to ever see a doctor. When I used to get physicals, she used to kid me about it. She called me a hypochondriac. She was a very private person, and I think she thought of her health as private, too. Even though we shared everything and didn't hide things from each other, that was the exception. That was one part of her life she didn't want to talk about."

Even the things she did for her health, she did in a way that protected her privacy. She would not jog or walk in public, but instead did circuits around the private tennis court at the Pearle home.

When she began suffering symptoms of ill health, she

never told anyone. It seems she would have taken that secret to her grave if she could have. But by 1994, she was suffering from an illness that was impossible to hide from her husband.

One night in Manhattan, they were heading back to their hotel and Elsie could barely walk because of abdominal pain. Stanley remembers telling her, "'Elsie, I'm going to take you to the doctor right now.' But no, she wouldn't do it, so we came home. She was very stubborn about her health."

Gary was very close to his mother, and he understood that she simply preferred to be the helper instead of the helped, to serve others rather than be served. "My mom was extremely private about illness or anything that might place a demand on someone else. As a result, she wasn't diagnosed with cancer until a very advanced stage."

Ultimately, her symptoms became so debilitating that Stanley had to carry her out of their home to a doctor's office, with Elsie insisting the entire way that she didn't want to go. It was the first time in her adult life—other than when she gave birth to her children—that she ever visited a physician.

That's when they discovered that Elsie had colon cancer. She underwent surgery to remove part of her colon. Coincidentally, the surgeon was one of the former Boy Scouts from the San Antonio troop that Stanley had volunteered with in 1940.

After the surgery, Elsie remained in a coma for several days. Her children joined Stanley to keep vigil at her bedside in the hospital.

In the midst of crisis, life sometimes offers a moment of comic relief. Gary and Linda were alone in the room with their mother when she suddenly awoke from her coma and said something unexpected.

"She said something that's not like her at all," Stanley says, chuckling softly. "She never used profanity and I didn't either."

Gary remembers the moment vividly: "She had the respirator on, and as she came to a sort of awareness the first thing she said was, 'Shit!' She usually had a strong sense of propriety. But it was a miracle that she was aware of her situation and verbalizing something about it."

The kids were overjoyed that their mother had made it back from the brink. After that, she grew better. It seemed like the surgery was a success. The doctor said it appeared that they'd removed all of the cancer, and for a while they were hopeful.

But about a year and a half later, Stanley had to half-carry a reluctant Elsie to a doctor's office again. That's when they discovered that the cancer had spread, and it had reached her liver. The doctor told them that she only had about six months to live.

Stanley wanted to tell the children, but his beloved "El" made him promise that he wouldn't tell them anything. "She was very stubborn about those kinds of things," he says. "She didn't want to worry them."

Although Gary was disappointed that his parents kept it a secret, he understood. "In effect she was asking my dad to carry the burden of that illness alone. Between the two of them, she was demanding a certain kind of loyalty of my dad, and boy did he give it. Those last two years were very important between them. He really walked through that anguish with her all alone. By the time they told us the cancer had recurred, she was in pretty bad shape."

Knowing Elsie's time was limited, the couple decided to make it as special as possible. One of the last things they did together was to take a cruise. Stanley remembers, "The last cruise we took was from Costa Rica on the Pacific side, through the Panama Canal to Curacao, ending up in Puerto Rico. Elsie almost didn't make it. She was dying, but she lived long enough to make that trip. It was difficult, but seeing the Panama Canal with her was a much more beautiful memory than traveling through it when I was in the service, missing her."

Although she didn't know how ill her mother was until the end, daughter Linda says it was clear that her parents' time together in those final months "was a very important time to her and to him."

When Stanley and Elsie finally told the children their mother was dying, they had just two weeks to say goodbye.

"She died beautifully, if there is such a thing as dying beautifully," Stanley says. "She was ready to go. She died at home in our bedroom. We had a beautiful home. The kids all came together, although Berta wasn't able to be there the night she died. But Elsie talked to all of them before she died. She was very close to all the children."

Linda remembers, "The only thing she was worried about or had a tear about was Dad. They had been together for so long. I reassured her we'd all take care of him."

Gary says, "It was my sister Linda that told my mother it was okay to go."

"I wasn't very good about talking to Elsie about it," Stanley says. "I didn't want to say goodbye. We'd never communicated that way. It takes a certain amount of bravery to say goodbye to somebody."

But after 57 years of marriage, perhaps Stanley and Elsie didn't need to exchange words. There was nothing hidden between the lifelong lovers, partners and best friends. Says Gary, "I remember that their last embrace was very powerful."

Stanley took comfort in one thing: "She died very peacefully, that I know. Gary is very spiritual and Linda is too, and he wouldn't let the undertaker take her away that night. We had a fireplace in our bedroom, where he lit candles and said a prayer. It was a very moving scene. It was a beautiful way to die."

Even so, after Elsie's death, Stanley spent plenty of time wrestling with anger, and he's never completely gotten over losing her. "I loved her very much and it was a terrible loss. I was kind of mad at her when she died, because I thought she could have lived longer if she wasn't so stubborn about going to the doctor. You shouldn't die from colon cancer—all you have to do is have a colonoscopy and check it out. I regret it very much because I could have had her a few more years. Those were the wonderful years of our life, too, because we were successful financially, and we were able to travel and to enjoy the children in ways that we couldn't when they were growing up. That's the thing, is to be able to live a little longer when your children are grown and enjoy them and your grandchildren, without all the aches and pains of raising them. You just have all the pleasures, you know. So she missed some of that."

Elsie passed away in 1996. She was 77 years old.

Shortly before Elsie died, the Netherlands division of Pearle Vision had decided to have a new tulip named after her. Although she didn't live long enough to make it to the official naming ceremony in the Hague, she did get to pick the color of the tulip that would bear her name.

"They're her favorite color, which is passionate pink," Stanley says. "They're very pretty. She would have loved them."

Until Stanley moved from the family home into a retirement community, he used to order Elsie tulips for his garden every year. The children still order them for their homes each year; it's a lively, warm-colored, beautiful reminder each spring of the lively, warm, beautiful woman who gave so much to the world around her.

Sometimes, it's the little things that people miss. Bill Yost recalls, "One of the losses we suffered when Elsie went was that Stanley's wardrobe tended to go to pot. One day he said to me, 'Hey, have you seen that new clothing store down on

Mockingbird? It's one of those warehouse operations. I got some nice pants there for $25.' And I'm thinking, *Oh, Stanley, you can do better!* He could have had everything tailored."

Elsie, the partner he'd always admired for her sense of the beauties in life, had always tried to help Stanley look his best. These days, his children sometimes step in to rescue their father's wardrobe, taking him to finer stores like Nordstrom.

Beyond the little things, Elsie's death was an enormous loss to everyone who knew her. Family friend Dr. Wolf says, "Mrs. Pearle was truly one of the greatest ladies I have ever known. She was always looking for ways to make life better for the people around her."

While Stanley misses Elsie, he's not the type to despair or suffer from depression. He remains active and positive. Still quite the charming, dashing, elderly gentleman, he's apparently considered quite a catch by the senior widows of Dallas.

"After my mother died," says his son David, "widows came after him in droves, but he just wasn't interested. He almost had to stop socializing. There was always some subplot to get him together with someone."

Not that Stanley has gone into hiding. He says, "For the past three years, I've been keeping company with a lovely lady named Arlene Liebs, who I've known for many years. Her husband died several years ago after a very happy marriage. We have a very nice relationship."

Stanley and Arlene sometimes go out to the theatre, to dinner or to parties. His children encourage the relationship. They like Arlene and are grateful that their father has someone in his life who encourages him to get out of his apartment, to be active and socialize.

Although he enjoys his time with Arlene, Stanley is content with the single life. "I don't mind being alone. Some men or women, when they lose their spouse, they get married right away because they're so used to having somebody around. But I never thought that way. I was always comfortable being alone. Probably the fact that I'm close to the children and grandchildren makes a lot of difference."

But Dr. Pearle still thinks about Elsie every day. "She was a wonderful partner my whole life, and I still miss that. I miss her advice, because every move I made, every decision I made, was always with her. So I miss my partner, there's no question about it."

Looking at old photos of her, nearly 10 years after her death, Dr. Pearle's eyes still turn misty with the memory of his true love. "I loved her hair up," he says wistfully. "She didn't wear it up often, but I liked it that way very much."

The love affair of Stanley and Elsie Pearle lives on in the memories of the family, and sometimes in the voices of the grandchildren. Linda explains, "My daughter Debbie is the oldest grandchild. She called my father 'Honey' because that's what my mother called him. They always had a very loving relationship. Since then, all of the grandkids have picked up on the pet name."

Perhaps when his grandkids call Stanley "Honey," he still hears an echo of Elsie's voice, her way of still saying an occasional hello to the sweetheart who didn't know how to say goodbye.

Long Lost Brothers

IN THE LIFE OF AN OPTIMIST, grief is sometimes accompanied by gratitude. After Elsie passed away, Stanley was grateful to be reunited with the brother he'd long missed.

Once his twin brother retired from optometry, Merle's inability to get a license from the Texas Optometry Board could no longer keep them apart. In later years, the brothers spent more time together, and after Elsie died, the renewal of their friendship became an even more important source of strength and joy for Stanley.

In 1998, when Pearle Vision threw Stanley an 80th birthday bash, Dr. Merle Pearle, his younger brother by just one hour, was also invited. Together again, the pair stood side by side to blow out the candles on their cake. Afterward, in a letter to the party organizer, Merle described the event as "overwhelming…one of the happiest days of my life."

In 2002, the brothers decided that they didn't want to be separated any longer. Now that Merle had retired and his children had moved away, Stanley encouraged Merle and his wife Ruth to move to Dallas. That move completed the reunion of the twins who had once been so inseparable, and closed one of the few disappointing chapters in Stanley's life.

"That was one of the nicest things that happened in my life, to have him close to me," Stanley says. "But we lost a lot of years together and I was very sad that I couldn't spend more of my life with him. We were very close. He was a very warm, sensitive person and we had a wonderful relationship."

Unfortunately, Merle's health was also very sensitive, and he ultimately died of kidney failure in early 2004, at the age of 85. Stanley was sad to lose his brother, but grateful that they were able to share those last days together.

Merle's widow still lives next door to Stanley in their retirement community and the two remain friends.

Although Merle and Stanley missed a lot of time together through their life, they got together when they could and created important memories that still make Stanley smile. He remembers one time when Merle came to visit him in Dallas, back in the '60s or '70s. As often happens with Stanley and his friends, they bonded over sports. For once in Stanley's life, the game did not go smoothly.

Stanley was typically an avid tennis player at his country club, but he was happy to indulge his brother with a game of golf, which was more Merle's speed. Stanley drove the cart, and at one hole, as his son David tells the story, he forgot to set the brake—although Stanley prefers to say that the brake failed.

Either way, the cart ran away with their clubs, careening down a hill to splash into a small lake at the bottom of the green.

"That was the last time I ever golfed," Stanley says with a chuckle.

"There was a little rivalry between the tennis players and the golfers at the club," recalls David. "The golfers never let Dad forget that he sent a runaway cart into the lake."

Not that Stanley wanted to forget that day, which was one of the few times after he grew up that he got to share a day with his twin brother, one of the dearest people in his life.

"He was a more sensitive person than I was, more interested in the arts than I was, more musical than I was. I was the hard-driving businessman. We were very different. But that didn't matter. He was a great brother."

Chapter 7

Today and Tomorrow

AT 88, STANLEY PEARLE IS AS VITAL AS MANY MEN 20 years younger. He still plays an important role at Pearle Vision, stays actively interested in the lives of his four children, 10 grandchildren and eight great-grandchildren, remains keenly interested and involved in community and world issues, and keeps a sharp eye on his favorite baseball teams.

On the recommendation of his son, David, a respected cardiologist, Dr. Pearle stays in shape by working out with a personal trainer several times a week. He believes that's been a big contributor to his continuing good health.

He has never completely retired and still shows up at his Pearle Vision office in Dallas twice a week for a couple of hours—although the new company headquarters are in Cincinnati, Ohio. At the Dallas division, there's still a special parking place by the door with his name on it.

"The company continues to make my association with them very pleasant," he says. "They still consider me an honored person in the company."

With his personality as charismatic as ever and his insight into the business world still sharply honed, he continues to be an important presence at company gatherings and franchise meetings. He continues to keep his fingers on the pulse of consumer trends, and people in the optical field continue to seek his advice.

It's easy to see why people like having Dr. Pearle around. While he was being interviewed for this book, a small group of people walked by his office, and he couldn't resist poking his nose out of the door.

"Hey, what's going on?" he asked jovially. "Who are the visitors?"

Upon finding out that they were new hires, he gave them a classic Dr. Pearle welcome. For him, that's never about making a sophisticated speech designed to impress—just a simple "hello" in which his honest goodwill and warm interest in other people shines through.

"Welcome to the company… How are you doing? Wow, you should be a football player… Nice to see you all, good luck to you."

Dr. Pearle does consider himself 80 percent retired. But, as a man who's always been engaged with life, he's not the type to be at a loss for what to do with his increased free time.

"I enjoy retirement," he says. "These days, I don't travel as much, but I like to read and watch sporting events. My friend Arlene wants me to be more active than I want to be. She's younger than I am, in her mid-70s, and she's very active. She plays tennis and she's always trying to get me to go. I just say, 'Look, I'm just too old for you.'"

Dr. Pearle says that, as long as he's healthy, he's not disappointed with the idea that he's slowing down. He says it's important to enjoy each phase of life for what it has to offer. "This is a wonderful age to enjoy, just as every age is. You can appreciate things more and you enjoy lots of things. But every age has its benefits, you know."

To him, the biggest joy of this time in his life is his family. "I miss my partner. But on the other hand, it's made up a lot by the fact that I'm so close to the children."

Unfortunately, most of them aren't as close to "home" as he'd like. Linda is the only one who still lives in Dallas. She has four adult children and six grandchildren. David is a cardiologist and professor at Georgetown University. He and his wife have two grown children and two grandchildren.

After a successful career in theatre, Gary went back to school to get a PhD in psychology. He's now a therapist with a practice in Los Angeles, California. He and his wife have two children—one in high school and one in college.

After a successful stint running a small opera company, Roberta also opted for a career shift and is now a clinical nutritionist specializing in eating disorders. She works at a hospital in Boston. She's married and has two children in high school.

All of Dr. Pearle's sons and daughters call him regularly.

He is closest with his eldest son David, who phones him just about every day. "I think it's one of the few regrets of my dad's life that I live so far away," David says. "I broke those bonds of dependency pretty young."

But David enjoys their regular visits and daily phone calls. "When I call, we talk about everything: sports, my brother and sisters, family news, estate matters. He's just a man of tremendous character and I admire him tremendously. He's such a decent, honorable person. The more you get to know him, the more you like him."

For Dr. Pearle, the admiration is mutual. "All my children are wonderful children. They're interesting, too, because they're actually four very different personalities. It's kind of strange because you think that children coming from the same parents and the same environment would have a lot of similarities. But each of them is unique."

He respects those differences. While he might comment in one breath that he and David have so much in common, including a love of sports, in the next breath he'll speak with wondering admiration about how musical Gary is and how well he plays the piano—something they don't have in common at all.

"He takes pride in his children," says his friend, Dr. Wolf, "and he's always there for them when they have any problems."

These days, Dr. Pearle speaks proudly and animatedly—he's not the type to outright brag—about the accomplishments of his grandchildren as well.

"One of Gary's sons is a third-year student at Harvard," Dr. Pearle starts, and then he's on a roll. "He's so bright, it's scary. And he's in the Krokodiloes, Harvard's famous *a cappella* singing group. In the summer, they travel all over the world, to places like Japan and South America and Europe. David's son Andy is an orthopedic surgeon in New York and a team doctor for the New York Mets. And his daughter Lauren is a lawyer. So he has the ideal Jewish children."

Listen to him talk about the grandkids long enough and it's easy to lose track of who's who. But Dr. Pearle doesn't. As with all people, he has a knack for maintaining a unique relationship with each of his grandkids and great-grandkids, making each of them feel important to him as individuals.

He took Linda's grandson, Jeremy, with him to a recent

Pearle Vision franchise convention. Linda's daughter talked to Jeremy on the phone while they were there. "She told me he was having a wonderful time," Linda says. "They were up in their room having a hamburger together because they were not able to have breakfast together. That's because someone wanted to talk to my dad every minute."

Roberta's 16-year-old daughter is a baseball fanatic, just like "Honey"—as the grandkids all call their grandfather. Roberta says, "He used to play ball with her. She had her little bat, and he'd pitch to her. One time he proudly told me that she almost took his head off."

Roberta's son David is only 14, but Honey has already given him a few man-to-man talks. "He always tells him, 'Now David, I want to talk to you about what to look for when you get married…' And David says, 'I'm only 14, Honey, I don't know if I wanna have one of these chats.'"

Although Dr. Pearle doesn't believe in preaching to kids, he still enjoys sharing his ideas and philosophies with them. "I try and teach kids to enjoy each phase of their lives, to take advantage of it. But I'm not a great philosopher, just a little bit here and there. When you get to be a grandfather, you have a tendency to do that. Most of your advice isn't worth a damn anyway, but some of it is."

Roberta thinks her father simply believes in looking out for the people he loves. "He worries so about all of us. He's a good guy."

Between his large family and his continuing interest in work, you'd think that would make life full enough for a man approaching 90. But he also continues to keep up-to-date on the issues of the world at large by following the news and reading books on current events.

Now that he's retired, he also spends a lot more time keeping up with his favorite sports—mainly baseball. Until a few years ago, Dr. Pearle often went to spring training in Florida with David and his nephew Chuck. A few times, his brother Merle went along as well.

These days, he's more of an armchair fan. "I have two televisions—actually three—but two side-by-side in the living room. So I can watch two different sports and read at the same time."

Chuck isn't surprised. He says there are few baseball fans as dedicated as his Uncle Buddy. Chuck recalls that when he was a kid, his uncle sometimes made expensive, long-distance calls to Chuck's family home in Pittsburgh just to hear the Pirates game.

"We would literally put the phone down next to the radio so he could listen to it on the telephone. Or if he couldn't call that day, he would call the next day to talk about the game. And he didn't just want the score—he wanted the details. So if Roberto Clemente hit a home run, he would want to know what the count was, what the pitch was, where the ball went, *et cetera*."

Bill Yost recalls that when he used to visit Stanley's office, he always admired the large picture behind Stanley's desk. "It was a painting of the stands at a baseball game. I asked Stanley, 'Why do you have that picture up there?' And he said, 'I'm nuts about baseball.' He was known to fly on a plane, see a game in Pittsburgh and fly back to Dallas."

Dr. Pearle is still a big baseball fan. He likes the Texas Rangers and the Boston Red Sox, "but I follow the Red Sox mainly because my daughter and grandchildren like them. And I'm originally from Pittsburgh, so I root for the Pittsburgh Pirates. They're pretty bad," he adds mildly.

The Pittsburgh Pirates aside, Dr. Pearle believes his life is a story of good fortune, just as much as it is the story of a man *making* his fortune. "You have to have a little bit of luck in your life, too. And I've had much more than my share of it.

You don't want to belittle the fact that you need to be a little lucky, because sometimes the slightest little change in your life could have a tremendous effect."

He not only thinks he's lucky to have made a success of his business. He thinks he's been lucky from the beginning, in all aspects of his life. "I think I was so fortunate in the fact that I had a wonderful childhood, even though we didn't have a lot of money. Even though I didn't have a father, I had uncles. I was active in Scouts. I had a great brother and we were very close. I was fortunate enough to get a job and then go to optometry school. I happened to meet a girl who turned out to be wonderful. I have a wonderful, healthy family. I've been able to travel a lot. I still have my health. I just think a person could hardly be any luckier than I am, and I am just full of gratitude.

"There are a few things that happened that could have been better, like losing Elsie. And I regret that all my children don't live close by. But we're still very close. If people were all as lucky as I've been, it would be a better world."

It might also be said that Stanley Pearle's ability to recognize and appreciate his own good fortune is part of what has made him successful. By creating a successful worldview, he has been more clearly able to identify opportunities as they have arisen, and has had enough belief in himself and his ideas to move forward on his dreams. With such an attitude, he has always been poised to see all the positive options, and to take advantage of them.

Into the Future

DR. PEARLE RECOGNIZES THAT THE OPPORTUNITY for long-term correction of near-sightedness through laser surgery often eliminates the need for either eyeglasses or contact lenses. But even though that could theoretically be bad for the optical business, as a true altruist, he fully supports any opportunity for people to improve their vision.

"I think it's good," he says simply. "I'm not supposed to like it so much, being in the optical field, because people get rid of their glasses, and normally near-sighted people are the best customers because they need glasses all the time. But it's a great option for people and the success rate is very good. Besides, people will always need glasses for reading."

Three of Dr. Pearle's children have had laser vision correction. Gary is the only holdout, but Dr. Pearle says that's only because his youngest son is especially meticulous about checking into all the pros and cons before taking any big step. Apparently, Gary is now thinking about undergoing the surgery as well.

Unlike his children, Dr. Pearle has nearly perfect distance vision, even at age 87. He didn't even need reading glasses until he was in his 50s, which also makes him quite different from most people.

Now that he wears them, he takes full advantage of modern innovations in eyewear. That is, his glasses are progressive bifocals and they're photosensitive—meaning that they darken in sunlight to reduce glare and provide protection against ultraviolet rays.

Dr. Pearle believes that, in spite of laser surgery, there's still plenty of room for the optical industry to grow by taking advantage of the ever-changing needs and wants of a consumer society. Nearly 100 percent of all people start to need reading glasses sometime in their 40s, when they commonly develop presbyopia.

So, sooner or later, nearly every American is a potential optical customer. Certainly the aging of the Baby Boomers has increased the sales margin on reading glasses.

Although there have been many recent innovations in the

field of vision care, there are always new challenges. As people live longer, they're developing more vision problems, such as macular degeneration, which is associated with advancing age. That's where organizations like the Pearle Vision Foundation come in with research funding.

Dr. Pearle expects the vision needs of the American public to continue changing. "The concept of vision itself has been altered in recent years by dramatic changes in modern lifestyles. We use our eyes quite differently than when I started in this field. Visual problems today are often caused by environmental influences, such as over-stimulation from television, eye strain from computer monitors and irritation from pollution."

He believes that the optical companies that do well in the future will be those that can stay on top of these kinds of changes and come up with new strategies to address them.

When Dr. Pearle envisions the Pearle Vision of the future, he sees an even more all-inclusive shopping place for eye care. "Eventually, I would hope that the Pearle brand would include not only optometric services, but ophthalmologic services as well. I think the name could grow to be the place you'd go for any optical needs that you have, including surgery and Lasik laser vision correction and all that."

Although fashion is king at the moment, Dr. Pearle says that style is not the only aspect of the optical field that's changing for the better. "The professionalism is a lot more advanced than it used to be. The quality of both the optometrists and the opticians is a lot better today."

The educational requirements to become an optometrist have certainly increased. Dr. Pearle was not required to get an undergraduate degree to get into optometry school, and he finished his program in three years. Today, becoming an optometrist usually requires a four-year bachelor's degree, followed by four years in optometry school—a total of eight years of study.

When Dr. Pearle first entered the profession, health insurance was not as prevalent as it is today, and vision care benefits were basically non-existent. Today, almost half the patients who visit Pearle Vision have some kind of eye care benefit as part of a comprehensive health insurance plan.

The health insurance trend is one thing that Dr. Pearle believes is giving a boost to his colleagues in private practices. In fact, a group of independent optometrists and ophthalmologists has founded a managed vision care company known as Vision Service Provider (VSP), which has become one of the nation's largest managed vision care companies.

Many businesses provide vision benefits to their employees through VSP. Plan members can only use approved VSP network providers, which include only independent optometrists and ophthalmologists. Optometrists who work for optical companies or own optical company franchises cannot take part in the plan.

Dr. Pearle explains, "Any doctor who is involved with a retail optical chain is not allowed to be a part of the VSP panel of providers. And VSP is very big. As a matter of fact, if it weren't for that, the independents would have a hell of a time existing. So that's good for the independents, but it creates yet another area of competition between the so-called independent providers and the company-hired or franchise providers. With almost 50 percent of working people having some sort of vision benefit, it's a very big item they're competing for. That's a very big change in the field today."

He acknowledges that, in the vision field, there continues to be tension between independent optometrists in private practice and large optical companies. "The competition is very severe. I think that probably will make it tough for some independent optometrists. Some very big, profitable corporations are involved that never used to be, and they have the capital to do whatever it takes to attract the consumer. When I first started, it was all local entrepreneurs. On the other hand, there will always be people who prefer to go to independent service providers. I think they'll both exist in the future."

One thing Dr. Pearle doesn't think will ever change is the public's desire for quality and service. He's glad to see that Pearle Vision's new parent company is working to reinvigorate its entire system with an even stronger commitment to that ideology.

At its 790 stores, the company did nearly $600 million in sales in 2005. Dr. Pearle says that those numbers are not nearly as big as they should be. But he believes that Luxottica is just getting started on a major shift in focus that will increase profits. He says that one of the most important tasks the new company is working on is unifying the franchises so that they have consistent policies and consistent service.

Another important task is marketing—deciding on the kind of customers Pearle Vision should target, then delivering a simple message. In Pearle Vision's case, Luxottica is looking for customers who put a high value on service and comfort; the company is promising those customers something it calls a "total eye care experience," which includes both a quality exam and an enjoyable shopping experience.

Overall, Dr. Pearle thinks that most of the changes, both at Pearle Vision and in the optical field in general, are for the better. "Consumers have much better choices now than they used to have, and they're getting much better care than they used to get. In general, the trends in the field benefit the consumer. From a personal standpoint, I'm proud and gratified that Pearle has been a part of it."

Success would have meant little to Stanley Pearle if it had not benefited his family. He was able to provide a comfortable life for his children and give them better educations and opportunities than he ever had, which is every good parent's dream.

But it was the way he and Elsie walked the road through their success that had the most lasting effect on their children's lives. Stanley and Elsie were role models who never took what they had for granted, and gave back as much as they received. They never forgot their values, and inspired their children to become the best they could be.

About the Author

CARA LOPEZ LEE BEGAN HER WRITING career in 1990 as a television reporter in Alaska, where she received 11 awards for outstanding journalism. Since then she has written and field produced for The Discovery Health Channel, The Food Network and Home & Garden TV. Her travel articles have appeared in such newspapers as *The Los Angeles Times* and *The Rocky Mountain News. A Man of Vision* is her first book.